INTO THE

Promised

Land

Desperately Seeking the Presence of God
In the Wilderness on Your Journey
into the Promised Land!

by

Stephanie D. Moore

Published by
Moore Marketing and Communications
Oklahoma City, Oklahoma
www.StephanieDMoore.com
www.MooreToRead.com

Bulk copies or group sales of this book are available by contacting
moore@stephaniedmoore.com or by calling (405) 306-9833.

FIRST EDITION PRINTED FEBRUARY 2017
Printed in USA

Moore, Stephanie D.
Into the Promised Land: 31-Day Devotional
First Edition.

Library of Congress Control Number: 2017902472
1. Jesus 2. Promise 3. Devotional 4. Spirituality 5. Religion 6. Christianity 7. God

Issued also as an ebook.

ISBN: 978-0-9962040-0-2

Into the Promised Land

Devotionals

The Promise	5
Day 1: A Broken Heart	7
Day 2: Tired	11
Day 3: Hope	17
Day 4: Thankful	21
Day 5: Love	27
Day 6: The Greatest Regret	31
Day 7: Loneliness	37
Day 8: Unhealthy	41
Day 9: Poor, Angry and Making Bad Choices	47
Day 10: God Heals	51
Day 11: Forgiveness	55
Day 12: Loveliness	57
Day 13: This Was Ordained	63
Day 14: Light	67
Day 15: Speak Life	73
Day 16: Loving Myself	77
Day 17: Honor	81
Day 18: Heart Words	85
Day 19: Grumpy	89
Day 20: Bad Days	93
Day 21: Words of Affirmation	97
Day 22: Instead of the Pain	101
Day 23: Prepared	105
Day 24: Thankful to God	109
Day 25: Poor Friends	113
Day 26: Environment	119
Day 27: Emotion	123
Day 28: My Routine	129
Day 29: Loving Me	133
Day 30: My God is Able	137
Day 31: The Everlasting Love of God	143
Into the Promised Land	149
About the Author	151

"But those who hope in the LORD will renew their strength.
They will soar on wings like eagles; they will run and not grow weary,
they will walk and not be faint."
Isaiah 40:31

INTO THE
Promised Land

The Promise

Moses my servant is dead; now therefore arise, go over this Jordan, thou, and all this people, unto the land which I do give to them, even to the children of Israel. Every place that the sole of your foot shall tread upon, that have I given unto you, as I said unto Moses. From the wilderness and this Lebanon even unto the great river, the river Euphrates, all the land of the Hittites, and unto the great sea toward the going down of the sun, shall be your coast. There shall not any man be able to stand before thee all the days of thy life: as I was with Moses, so I will be with thee: I will not fail thee, nor forsake thee." Joshua 1:2-5

God has made several promises to us concerning our future. Often times, when God is bringing us out of bondage, we see our worst days in abundance before we make it to our promised land. Nothing will ever separate us from God's love. While we may not feel his presence, he is present. The teacher never speaks during the test, have faith. God is with you. There are so many stories in the Bible that confirm, our best days are always ahead of us. Consider the servant Joseph: sold into slavery by his brothers, betrayed by a leader he was loyal to, wrongfully imprisoned and seemingly forgotten... only to rise in power and become second in command to Pharaoh, the ruler of Egypt. He was developed, mature, emotionally stable and ready to serve in leadership by the time his purpose manifested itself.

You may have been doing everything God has asked you to do, waiting in patience, believing for the best but nothing has manifested, nothing has changed and in fact, it's gotten worse. Don't worry! Trust God, he is faithful! Don't complain while you are in the wilderness because your promised land is just around the corner.

Into the Promised Land

DAY
1

A Broken Heart

"The LORD is close to the brokenhearted
and saves those who are crushed in spirit." Psalm 34:18

In Context

David is so thankful to God for blessing him and protecting him. In this chapter, as he runs from his son, Abimelech, who wishes to take over his kingdom, David says, "I will bless God every chance I get!" He goes on to express how God alleviated his fears. He encourages the reader to look at God and give him a smile, that we should never hide how we feel before God. He then testifies how God has always gotten him out of a tight spot and how God's angels encamp around us when we pray. He then dares us to taste and see the goodness of God. He adds, worship God if you want the best, that worship opens the door to God's best. He then adds that those who worship God are full of his Word and honor him with their actions. That when we are good (and good to others), God watches over. God won't tolerate repeat sinners, he will get rid of them quick. David also shares that if you are crying for help, God hears you and desires to rescue you. That if you are suffering from a broken heart, he is right there to help. People that worship God are not absent from persecution, but they are in the company of God – he is protecting each and every aspect of their person. The wicked commit slow suicide; they waste their lives hating good people. God pays for each slaves freedom and no one who comes to God is lost.

A BITTER WEEPING FOR WHAT HAS BEEN LOST

Have you ever been fired? Well, I have! But on this instance, I was laid off. I had a prominent position with a local television station

7

as their marketing coordinator. I worked hard too. I made sure our website was updated daily, our social media sites were updated, our print ads and schedule were correct, digital billboards running the right schedule, worked with local colleges to make sure their teams competing on our game show were in compliance, negotiated our website design, communicated with our syndicated programs to secure prizes to give away during our game show, sold advertising,, created graphics, and trained our new on-air designers were proficient using the graphics system on our new boards in the control room. I loved that every day I came into work, there was a different area I could work in. I was an independent worker and a creative thinker with new ideas.

One day, while at the State Fair of Oklahoma, helping facilitate contestants and audience members for a cooking segment with Oklahoma Natural Gas, a co-worker shared we were going to get laid off later that day. I knew something was going on because we weren't spending our marketing dollars as before but hadn't realized layoffs would occur. No later had she told me that I received an e-mail asking me to report to HR at 3 pm.

I loved my job and I could have worked for another station… but we were one of the only broadcast stations in the market that did not air news. I preferred not to work in news (murder, fires, kidnapping/disappearing) it was too much drama and somewhat depressing.

I was heartbroken and lost all in one. I didn't know what to do or where to go. I had my own business, and all I heard God ask me was did I trust him. Of course I did, but what in the world was I going to do? I had car insurance, rent, 2 kids at home… so much. But I kept hearing, "Trust me" in my spirit. I did. I was lost for a little while in my broken-heartedness but eventually, I moved forward.

Those steps forward allowed me to become a campaign manager for a local candidate that went on to win his race with 73% of the vote. He was a great client for more than 2 years.

"The Lord doth build up Jerusalem: he gathereth together the outcasts of Israel. He healeth the broken in heart, and bindeth up their wounds." Psalm 147: 2-3

In Context

Psalm 147 opens with: It is good to praise God! Praise is beautiful and fitting. It shares that God rebuilds, gathers and heals. He is all knowledgeable and possesses limitless strength... that we could never grasp how much he knows or does. He puts the fallen on their feet and pushes the wicked into a ditch. Praise God with thanksgiving, song and music because it is he that prepares the sky for rain, places grass on the mountains feeding cattle and crows. That he is not intimidated or impressed by any amount of power but those that fear God get his attention. Praise God! He has made us secure, blessed our families, keeps the peace and puts the best bread on our table. His promises are headed our way, quickly and efficiently. He has the power of nature within his realm. He speaks to us to clearly and assertively as he has never done with anyone else before. Praise God!

Final Notes

God is faithful. He knows that what you are going through is extremely painful and almost unbearable. But, if you dare to trust him, even in this difficult season, he will grant you double for your trouble. Instead of asking why or when, ask what? What can I do to make today a better day as I transition to my next level? It's never a setback, but always a set up to take you higher and higher. God is doing a new thing in your life. Embrace it. Don't worry about who has walked away or who has betrayed your trust. God is still on the throne, let him pull you out of that ditch and you can wait and watch him throw them in the ditch. But, if it doesn't happen the way you desire, know he is taking care of you. When it seems like he is absent, he is working behind the scenes preparing a place just for you.

Prayer

Most Gracious and Heavenly Father, we have no idea why the pain we feel seems to be so unbearable. Our bodies are limp, our minds are fragile, our hearts are broken and our thoughts are toxic. Help us to believe in you. Help us to trust you. Help us to encourage ourselves as we wait to see the goodness of the Lord in the land of the living. Lord, you promised us that you would heal our broken hearts, that we could taste and see your goodness in our lives, that we could trust you to execute vengeance. While we don't want to hurt anyone, God we do ask that you shine a light on the pain that was caused and prick their hearts. Lord, help us to grow in love that we can pray to bless those that despitefully use us. Help us to guard our hearts and be wise enough to stop throwing our pearls to swine, to value ourselves and to expect your best. While we ask all these things, God we shout the highest praise to your Holy Name! You are an awesome God! We may not see you but we know you are working: protecting us, preparing a place for us and providing for us. Thank you. Restore in us a clean heart and a right spirit that we may serve you in wholeness and truth.
In Jesus Name, Amen.

DAY
2

Tired

"And when Rachel saw that she bare Jacob no children, Rachel envied her sister; and said unto Jacob, give me children, or else I die." Genesis 30:1

In Context

Rachel was favored by Jacob. She was his beautifully esteemed wife he'd worked a lifetime for. Even after her father tricked him into marrying her ugly sister, Jacob continued to work for her love. Finally, they were married but Rachel was barren. Her sister had several babies for Jacob and often teased Rachel because of it. Rachel was angry and upset. She cursed Jacob and yelled at him to give her children. Jacob responds - "Am I God? Am I the one who refused you babies?" Jacob wanted to have children with Rachel as much as she wanted to have them with Jacob. But, it wasn't her season. In her impatience, she gave Jacob her slave to have children with... and he did. She named both of the maids sons, Bilhah (Vindication) and Naphtali (Fight). Her sister, Leah, who was now barren responded by giving Jacob her maid to have children with. She too had a pair of sons named, Gad (Lucky) and Asher (Happy). One day, one of Leah's children offered her some mandrakes (a form of drug), Rachel asked Leah could she have some as well. But Leah was angry at Rachel for persuading Jacob to spend more time with her and said, "You already took my husband, now you want my son's mandrakes?" So, Rachel responded, "Ok, I will let Jacob sleep with you tonight if you allow me to have some of your son's mandrakes." So, when Jacob returned he slept with Leah and she became pregnant with her 5th son. She also had another son and daughter after. Their names were: Issachar

11

(Bartered), Zebulun (Honor) and Dinah (which means Avenged but is not revealed in scripture). Then God remembered Rachel and allowed her to have a son, Joseph (Add) and while she was having him she prayed for another child. After Joseph was born, Abraham wanted to take his family and move away. He'd worked more than 14 years for their father, and he argued his case to him. But Laban responded with, "I know that I have been blessed because of you, name your wages." Jacob came up with what he thought was a fair deal. But Laban intended to cheat Jacob. Fortunately, God allowed Jacob to balance the injustice with wisdom. He became rich as a result.

PATIENCE IN THE STORM

I have experienced some storms in my life. I have always prided myself in being obedient to God. But, that obedience (albeit not perfect) often led to periods of prolonged heartbreak and humility before any promotion or promised land seemed to appear.

One such instance included when I moved from Atlanta to DC. I knew without a doubt that God wanted me to move. He did not want me to remain in Atlanta. So, I did it. I quit my job, gave up my dream house, put my furniture in storage and left for DC with my two daughters. We didn't have anywhere to live and checked in to one of those Extended Stay hotels. The room was small. There was a hot plate, a refrigerator, a microwave and a toaster. I had my car, a Pontiac Grand Prix, my laptop and a handful of clothes. Dallas had her cello, Brooklyn her viola. We slept on one bed or one armchair (Dallas and I alternated on this chair, usually her) and the minimal cable and Internet that came with it. I had about $10,000 from my 401K. It paid for food, rent, cell phone bill, car payment and insurance... and lasted about 3 months.

I searched and searched and searched for a job. I almost had a great job a couple of times. I was at my wits end and penniless. It was Christmas Day and my oldest daughter Dallas would soon celebrate her 16th birthday. I promised her Golden Corral but was waiting on child support from her father to pay for it... $50. It never came. We instead drove mindlessly through the DMV streets as I cried and tried to resonate within myself that I had indeed heard from God.

Never did I doubt myself more. I was tired. I was angry. I wanted to fight but couldn't. My family made fun of me. They questioned my sanity. They thought less of me more and more each day. It was hard to have a high self esteem when those I loved the most seemed to abandon me at my weakest moments. I studied the Holy Spirit, I tried to start the prayer line God told me to start... never receiving one call. Despite leaving a million business cards with the prayer line everywhere. I was overwhelmed and defeated. I didn't understand.

Finally, I surrendered. I called my mother in law and asked her for help. I needed money or we would be homeless. She told me she would give me enough to get home but only if I promised to move back home. I did but I didn't want to. But... I had to. I thought that I had failed God. Did I do something wrong and he was angry with me? I thought I was doing what he wanted. Why was I forced to move back home?

When I got home, I was forced to stay with my sister and she made it clear she did not want me around. My daughters and I suffered in silence as I continued to try and find work. I was so humiliated. I was so tired. I was so over life. I wanted to die.

I can only imagine that this is exactly how Rachel felt. She knew that Jacob loved her, but here he was sleeping with her sister and having children by her. As she, his supposed prize, sat barren in a quiet household surrounded by proof he was leading a productive life. Rachel became bitter. She wanted to fight and that is exactly what she did. She told Jacob that she would die if he refused to give her children. Instead, she had children but died in childbirth.

As I write this, I am on assignment. Sitting in obedience but once again in a place of great humility. I am tired. I am trying not to get bitter. I don't want to die in childbirth. God help all of us.

"And Joseph said unto them, Fear not: for am I in the place of God? But as for you, ye thought evil against me; but God meant it unto good, to bring to pass, as it is this day, to save much people alive." Genesis 50: 19-20

In Context
Joseph was the first born son of Rachel. His brothers sold him into slavery and told his father that he was dead. They were jealous of Joseph because he was favored by his father and treated differently. While in slavery, Joseph served with excellence. He maintained a positive attitude and disposition despite being treated unfairly over and over again. Finally, one of the many people he helped remembered him during a troubling time in Egypt. Pharaoh had a horrible dream he could not interpret and Joseph was called upon. Joseph was not only endowed with the wisdom to interpret the man's dream, but he was also provided with the wisdom to solve the problem. Pharaoh appointed him a high position in the kingdom to execute his proposed plan that would save their people from famine. While he is supplying food to many of the people of Egypt, his brothers coming attempting to purchase food. The pain he felt was so deep that at first, Joseph refuses. His brothers don't recognize him, but he recognizes them! His heart is filled with sadness. He manipulates the situation so that they will be forced to bring his brother to Egypt. He wants to ensure that he did not meet a similar fate as himself. When they do bring him, he reveals his true identity to his brothers and asks them to bring his father and entire family to Egypt. This scripture describes a moment after his father passes away and his brothers are in fear that Joseph will retaliate and get them back. But instead, Joseph assures them that he understood God's purpose in it all and that it was more than about any of them, but a whole nation of people God sent him to save.

Final Notes
God wants to use us. He wants us to be available to his use in good times and bad times. He wants to be sure that we are open and available to follow his command even when we don't think we should have to. Sometimes, God has to take us really low (in one of the most humble and humiliating places) to lift us up. He will always get

the glory when a magnificent work is done in our lives. Thank God, bless his name and stay the course. God is not being silent, he is going ahead of you and preparing a place for you. Praise him in the process, endure the process, and move on through the process. The storm won't last forever and in the interim, he has sent the ravens to feed you and rained manna in your wilderness. Praise God for the blessing of prayer and his mercy. Keep moving forward believing for God's best, only faith pleases God.

Prayer
Most Gracious and Heavenly Father, thank you for life. Thank you for the air that we breathe. Thank you for shelter in the middle of our storm. Lord, we want to live a life that pleases you. We want to honor you with more than our words. We want to honor you with our hearts and hands. Lord, help us to continue in faith despite the immense pain we feel and the overwhelming spirit of defeat. Lord, shape our prayers with your desires, shape our words with your truths, shape our thoughts with your promises. Help us to sacrifice our pride and humble ourselves in true submission to you. Just as you found it not too little to humble yourself and join us in human form as Jesus Christ, we ask that you empower us with the undefeated spirit of humbleness and humility. Lord, remind us that we can trust you and that you are faithful. Remind us that you will never leave us nor forsake us. Lord help us to combat the spirit of denial, the spirit of rejection, the spirit of low self-esteem. Restore in us a faith that is stronger than any threat, mightier than any enemy and taller and wider than any obstacle we face. You are our God and we can trust you. We know that you are faithful and we choose today to believe! We will not die in childbirth. Instead we will mentally, emotionally and spiritually rise above every tactic of Satan to pull us down. We give you glory, honor and praise in the mighty and matchless name of Jesus Christ.
In Jesus Name, Amen.

DAY 3

Hope

"Many are saying of me, God will not deliver him. But you Lord, are a shield around me, my glory, the One who lifts my head high. I call out to the Lord, and he answers me from his holy mountain. I lie down and sleep; I wake again, because the Lord sustains me. I will not fear though tens of thousands assail me at every side." Psalm 3:2-6

In Context

Written as David fled his son, Abasalom, David opens with a simple question, "Lord, how many people rise up against me?" He adds the view by spectators depict his impending doom. But David, states that God is his deliverer and restorer - his shield and the one who hears his calls for help. He refuses to fear and recognizes that God is his sustenance. He then calls our, "Arise God and strike my enemies on the jaw - break the teeth of the wicked." From the Lord comes deliverance, may your blessing be upon your people.

<u>GOD WILL DELIVER YOU</u>

Have you ever had someone in your life that needed public recognition for every good thing they did? Someone that loved to be good to you while you were around but talked about you behind your back? I certainly have. When you chase God's purpose for your life people will question whether God is really for you and what you do if everything isn't happening the way they think it should.

I have always been a big investor. I spend more on my purpose that my daily living. From one leadership class to the next, I always end up in the hole. Whether it is the advertising, the venue, the swag bags, the meals or the contests - I always go over budget. My daily living

17

always pays the price. My phone may get cut off... or my water... or the Internet. My rent is always late. One year my car insurance lapsed after paying full coverage for seven years... Of course, then I had a car accident within days of the lapse. It was devestating.

To everyone else, from the outside looking in, I looked like a failure. But, from the inside looking out - I knew I was operating in the will of God. After so long, people began to whisper about me and abandon me. Even my family, my best friends and my favorite clients.

Their unbelief was so loud, I started listening to them instead of God. I almost gave up hope. But God called out to me in my darkest place and let me know, I wasn't alone.

3 years later and I still over-budget. I still struggle with personal finance but my ministry has served more than 600 kids! We help teenagers look at their daily choices differently, learning to value prayer and trust God. Our influence has even reached the Congo! I am pleased and excited... I have hope beyond circumstance.

"Joshua said to them, "Do not be afraid; do not be discouraged. Be strong and courageous. This is what the Lord will do to all the enemies you are going to fight," Joshua 10:25

In Context

Joshua and his soldiers fought the battle of Jericho and defeated AI. The king of Jerusalem heard of his success and that a larger and stronger city (Gibeon) than AI had entered a peace treaty with Joshua. The king was shocked because Gibeon was a big city!

So the king created a pact with four other kings from Hebron, Jarmuth, Lachish and Eglon. They positioned themselves and attacked Gibeon. Gibeon sent word to Joshua and begged assistance. Joshua marched up with his entire army as God revealed, "Do not be afraid. I have given them into your hand. Not one of them will be able to withstand you."

Joshua and his army surprise attacked them. They were unready and confused. They ran and fled and God rained down hailstones. More of them died by hail than by the hand of Joshua. During the battle, Joshua called out to God and asked him to make the sun stand still AND it did! It stayed long enough for them to avenge themselves of their enemies.

However, the five kings managed to escape to a cave. When Joshua found out, he had his soldiers block them in with rocks and stand guard. He also insisted they continue fighting their enemies. He encouraged them to attack them from the rear and keep them our of their cities. God promised the victory.

The army continued to attack but a few men reached their cities. His entire army was safe and sound. Joshua then commanded they roll away the stones that kept the kings captive. Once the kings were brought out of the cave, Joshua commanded that each army commander place a knee on a kings neck. He then told them to be strong and courageous that this is what God would do to all of their enemies. The he put the kings to death and hung their bodies on poles all night. At daybreak, they threw the bodies back in the cave and rolled the stones back in front of the opening.

Joshua and his army went on to defeat and utterly destroy every person in Makkedah, Libnah, Lachish, Eglon and Debir. He subdued the whole region and their kings. He left no survivors... just as God commanded. All these kings and their lands Joshua conquered in one campaign because God fought for Israel.

Final Notes
We may be surrounded by people that desire to see us fail or even worse - plan to destroy us. But we have to believe and hope in God who will never fail us. He sees the plots and plans of the enemy and he will utterly destroy them for us and before us. We don't have to worry - we will sleep well at night knowing we are safe in God's hands.

Prayer

Lord Jesus! Thank you for being so good to us! Thank you for blessing us and keeping us. Thank you for your protection. Strengthen us Lord. Help us to chase and utterly destroy our enemies as you desire. Keep us in perfect peace as we obey your every command. Be with us and keep your hands of protection, direction and provision and blessing upon us. Forgive us of our sins and help us to trust you when all looks dim.
We are more than conquerors through Christ Jesus!
In Jesus Name, Amen.

Thankful

"In everything give thanks:
for this is the will of God in Christ Jesus concerning you."
I Thessalonians 5:18

In Context

I Thessalonians 5 breaks down some of the core principals of living as a true child of God. It insists that we stay ready because Jesus will come as a thief in the night. We are called to be watchful and sober-minded: to continue our work as the light. It calls us to wear the breastplate of faith and love (righteousness) and the helmet (protecting our thoughts and subsequent actions) with salvation in mind. It is not our job to avenge – it is our job to love and obtain salvation.

We are called to comfort one another and love one another, know those that labour in the Lord among us, recognize those in authority over us and esteem them highly in love for their works sake. We must be at peace among ourselves. We are also called to warn those that are unruly, comfort those that are feeble minded, support the weak and be patient toward all men. Vigilante justice is looked down upon and embracing the goodness in all is highly esteemed. Rejoice. Pray Always. Give thanks in every situation for this is the will of God toward us. We are not to quench the Holy Spirit and embrace prophesy. Prove all things, hold fast to that which is good. We must shy away from evil and allow God to cleanse us spirit, soul and body. That he may present you blameless when our savior returns. God IS faithful and he WILL do it. Pray for our leaders and greet all brethren with a holy kiss. Share this with all brethren and the grace of God be with you.

FLAWLESS

I was blessed to have a heart-to-heart with my mom one afternoon. She said, "Stephanie, you always seem so happy on Facebook. You need to let people see the other side too." I responded, "Mama, nobody wants to hear about your fears and tears, they want the happy and positive stuff." She said, "Be real. Be you."

The truth is, I work hard. I think I am always working. I dream about work. Someone once told me, "Stephanie - you love to work. That's what you love." But, I don't think that's it. No, I like to help people. I really like to help people. I like when people have a better outlook or a better day. I like it when people transition from helpless and hopeless to hopeful and grateful. I love to smile and see other people smile. I believe in doing a job right with integrity and being brutally honest even when it hurts.

I am not perfect. My life is not perfect. My God is. I trust him. I have been homeless. I have had every utility shut off at some point. I have had to beg for rides to work because I don't have gas money or a car functioning to do so. I am not rich. I am not even affluent. I live check to check.

When God asks me to do something that is seemingly bigger than me - bigger than I normally think, I ALWAYS hesitate but I say, YES. You see, I know that if God asks me to do it - he is going to make it happen. I don't need to just show the good, but I have to show the real.

I am trying to do things bigger than me and that is real. I can't do it alone, but I know God is sending his soldiers to the front line to help because this is all about what he wants.

Yes. He is FLAWLESS and in the words of Beyoncé, I woke up like this, FLAWLESS. (God doesn't make mistakes.) Be encouraged. Every day doesn't feel good but it is good.

"Is anything too hard for the Lord? At the time appointed I will return unto thee according to the time of life and Sarah shall have a son." Genesis 18:14

In Context

Chapter 18 opens with "And the Lord appeared unto him…" This phrase immediately lets us know that Abraham was in the presence of God. Suddenly, when Abraham looked up, three men stood by him. Abraham immediately ran to them and bowed down before them. He begged the man to stay a while that he may wash their feet and they might rest. He asked if he could feed them too. Then he rushed into his tent and asked his wife to prepare a meal. Then he ran to get his best meat to have prepared for them. Once the meat was ready he added butter and milk and set it before them. They ate.

Then they asked where is your wife? He told them that she was in the tent. She was standing within ear shot when the Lord shared with Abraham and Sarah that they would have a son. When Sarah heard it, she laughed. She laughed because she and Abraham were so old their bodies couldn't physically handle or create life. She said, "After I have waxed old shall I have pleasure, my Lord being old also?"

Then the Lord questioned Abraham about Sarah's laughter and comment. He then stated, "Is anything too hard for the Lord?" Sarah afraid, denied laughing but God replied, "No, you did laugh." The three angels then got up and looked toward Sodom where they planned an impending doom. The people of Sodom and Gomorrah cried loud and hard because the sins committed there were so hideous. They were going to witness with their own eyes what the people had been crying about. Before they left Abraham, they discussed among themselves as to whether they should share with Abraham what would occur. As they discussed it, they asked if they should share this with Abraham being that he would become a mighty nation (a response directly related to the promise they just made he and Sarah). They continued, because they KNEW Abraham and that he will continue to teach his family to worship and honor God and be just. (How amazing for God to say). So, they told Abraham the plan. But, Abraham stood before the Lord. Then he

began to ask about the innocent God fearing people, would they
die as well? The angels assured him that if there was 50 good men,
they would not kill them. Abraham, fearful that the number was too
large, asked, what about 40 or 30 or 20… when the angels agreed
at each quantity they would spare, Abraham was relieved but not
satisfied. He asked once more and prayed he did not make them
angry in his insistence. What if there were only 10? The angels
agreed they would save 10, left Abraham and journeyed down to
Sodom and Gomorrah.

Final Notes
Sometimes we are called to suffer long and hard. We are still
expected to be grateful and thankful to God in every circumstance.
Sarah and Abraham believed God's promise long before it came to
pass. Their hope became dismal and almost non-existent when it
really came to pass because they'd suffered so long and hard that
Sarah laughed when they reminded them of the promise. It had
been a long journey and one that she determined was futile. When
she heard the seriousness of God and why she questioned his words
of truth, she grew fearful. She knew the prophesy was real. The
trinity Godhead trusted and admired the faith of Abraham so much
they not only guaranteed he was the father of many nations but they
respected him for caring for his family in such a way. This respect
caused them to stop and allow Abraham to be aware of what was
going to transpire where his nephew and family lived. Abraham
stood before the Lord and begged for the survival of good God-
fearing people in the land they intended to destroy. God knows you.
He knows that you believe him. He knows that you trust him. He
knows that your faith is becoming thin and that it may not be gone,
but you too would laugh if he were to repeat his promise today.
Stay in faith. God is faithful. Thank him for his faithfulness. He
sees your tears and he knows your pain. He will do what he said he
would do… just believe.

Prayer

Lord Jesus, please help our unbelief. Help us to hold tightly to our faith as if it were our last breath. Some of us are weary and don't know how to lift our heads or dry the never ending tears that fall violently from our eyes. We need you now more than ever to strengthen us and help us survive the pain we feel. Lord, we confess we don't know or understand everything that is happening to us. We can't compare our apples to your oranges because we don't know what your plan looks like. We know that you are strategic and good. So Lord, we pray right now in the name of Jesus that you heal our broken hearts and help our unbelief. Help us to have faith, confess our faith, walk in our faith and run in faith. Lord, help us to be strong and courageous for we will not stay in this wilderness. We are walking valiantly into our promised land. Thank you for loving us in spite of us, in the mighty and magnificent name of Jesus.
In Jesus Name, Amen.

DAY
5

Love

"But I will sacrifice unto thee with the voice of thanksgiving; I will pay that I have vowed. Salvation is of the Lord. And the Lord spake unto the fish, and it vomited out Jonah upon the dry land."
Jonah 2:9

In Context

Jonah was a messenger of God called to speak to a place called Nineveh. Nineveh was evil. They did horrible things and God sent Jonah to warn them. But Jonah, knowing God would forgive them, refused to go. Instead, he went the other direction and boarded a ship to go and get as far away as he could. The ship he boards finds itself in a storm. The men on the ship pray to their gods and wake Jonah amidst the storm. They ask him to pray to his God, that they might not perish. They cast lots and discover the root of their issue is coming from him. They ask his business on the boat and about his occupation. Jonah confides that he fears the Lord and has been running from his instruction. He tells them to throw him off the ship. Instead, they try their best to make it to the shore with Jonah on board... but they can't. So they begin praying and asking for God's mercy that they don't die with Jonah. They throw him off the ship, make vows and sacrifice to God as the sea calms. Jonah is swallowed by a whale and is in the belly three days and nights. While in the belly of the whale, Jonah begins to pray. He prays, I am cast out of your sight, yet, I will look again toward your holy temple. When My soul fainted within me, I remembered the Lord and my prayers were heard in his holy temple. They that observe lying vanities forsake their own mercy. But, I will speak in gratitude and pay thee what I vowed, salvation comes from you. And the Lord spoke to the fish and it

27

vomited Jonah on dry land.

LOVE IS SACRIFICE

There was a time in my life when the last thing I wanted to do was what God told me. I had so many other wonderful ways to praise and serve God, why this? God wanted me to serve someone that hurt me very deeply and in a profound way. Initially, I said yes. I will obey. But, as time progressed, I didn't see a change in the person and the persecution only seemed to become greater and overbearing. At first, I tried to "warn" the person that things were becoming a bit too much for me and I was considering walking away. This only seemed to worsen the situation. I quit. Against the will of God, I was done. My heart was broken, I'd been lied to, disrespected and hurt... God certainly didn't intend for me to go through this right? I couldn't be a doormat!

Within weeks my life fell a part. Bills were due, money was fleeting, work was scarce and those that did hire me weren't remitting payment. Everyone I loved and trusted turned their back on me. What in the world was going on?

After a month or so, I began to hear crazy messages about repentance and obedience. Ironically enough, I'd just finished my book, 'Obey: Obedience Breaks Every Yoke: Nothing is bigger than our God', when all of this began.

God told me again, "Go back. I want all of my children to have salvation and you have to help him." What? Me? Why me? Doesn't he have any other Christian friends that can bring him to salvation? I asked out loud. I immediately heard God say, "Yes, but I want it to be you. You promised me you would live for me and this is what I want." God was right. I did make that promise and until this assignment, others were difficult and mind-blowing but this was excruciating. I mean this particular person I'd cried endlessly over and for, praying for their deliverance and mine when I became less tolerant and less Jesus and more Stephanie.

God then shared that he wanted me to be happy. That his goal was not to torture me but to strengthen my trust in him. When times got hard he insisted I give any and every situation over to him. Let him work it out. That way the emotional heaviness I was trying to carry could be lifted off my shoulders and subsequent actions could be gentle, peaceful and spirit giving instead of bitter, angry and resentful.

"As for me, I will call upon God; and the Lord shall save me." Psalms 55:16

In Context

David writes about the wrath of his enemy and calls on the Lord for help. He says "fearfulness and trembling come upon me" and compares the feeling to horror. But later he clarifies that the enemy was his close friend, someone that he cares for and spent time in church with. He gets so angry at the thought that he prays God's vengeance on them. He shares that they refuse to change even though God has given them time to change. That instead they speak sweetly to David but are secretly at war with him. But David casts his care upon the Lord who he trusts to avenge and destroy.

Final Notes

Obedience is love... love for God. How can we have a table prepared in the presence of our enemies if we aren't on the battlefield. God wants to show his love for all people and his strength in battle for his people. He wants his children to reflect his love, patience, endurance and thoughtfulness as he executes judgment and subsequent punishment. We can trust God to protect us, the question is can he trust us to be obedient?

Prayer

Most Gracious and Heavenly Father, please help us to reflect you and only you as we are obedient to your will. Remind us often that to obey you is to love you. Help us to mature and enjoy basking in your presence despite opposition and betrayal. Help us to love our fellow man and forgive them as you have forgiven us. Help us to also be sure to cast every hurt, pain, negative emotion and struggle into your hands. We know this situation is for your glory, for your honor, for your recognition. We will not be slight in giving you the praise! We thank you, we trust you, we love you.

In Jesus Name, Amen.

The Greatest Regret

"While he was still speaking a crowd came up, and the man who was called Judas, one of the Twelve, was leading them. He approached Jesus to kiss him, but Jesus asked him, "Judas, are you betraying the Son of Man with a kiss?"
Luke 22:47-48

In Context

Judas, one of the twelve disciples of Jesus, agreed to betray Jesus with temple leaders for a sum of money when no one was looking. Soon it was time to honor the Passover, and Jesus asked the disciples to prepare for it by reaching out to a local man they would see when they entered the city. He had a room for them to honor Passover.

Jesus greatly desired to spend this time with them. He vowed not to eat or drink again until the Kingdom of God comes. He then instructed them to remember him often by giving thanks when breaking and eating the bread, which represented his body and afterward, drinking the wine, which represented his blood. At this point he admitted that one of them would betray him and it would end poorly for that man.

The disciples wondered which of them would do such a thing and began to argue who was the greatest. Jesus interrupted them by teaching that a true leader is the one who sits at the table, yet he is the most humble and serving among them. He assured them that just as God trusted him to teach the kingdom, they to have been trusted to teach it and that as he goes to sit at the table with his father, they too will sit at the table to judge the twelve tribes of Israel.

He then shares with Peter that he will face many trials. That he had prayed his faith will not fail. But Peter denies it could happen, that he would die or even go to jail for Jesus. Jesus responds that Peter will deny him three times before the rooster crows that day.

He then asked them if he ever sent them out without adequate provision. They respond, "Never." He then instructs them to sell their coat if they need to but to make sure they had a purse, a bag and sword because the prophecy stated he would be numbered among transgressors. They showed him their two swords, and he responded, "That's enough."

Jesus then went to the Mount of Olives to pray. He instructed them, "Pray that you do not fall into temptation." He then went a short distance and began to pray. He was very distraught yet obedient. He prayed that his cup be taken away but if not, the Lord's will be done. An angel came and strengthened him. He later returned to find them sleeping due to exhaust from sorrow and said again, "Why are you sleeping? Pray that you do not fall into temptation."

At that very moment Judas arrives with temple leaders and attempts to kiss Jesus. Jesus asks, "Judas, are you betraying the Son of Man with a kiss?" At that moment one of his disciples cuts one of the attending soldiers' ear off. But Jesus heals the man and states, "No more of this." He then asks the temple leaders if he is leading a rebellion to be approached in such a way. That he spent every day with them in the temple courts... but this was their day of darkness.

They took Jesus to the house of the high priest, Peter followed at a distance. Within an hour, Peter was accused of being a follower of Jesus - which he denied at every accusation. After the third, a rooster crows and a Peters heart breaks as he recalls Jesus' words from before.

Jesus is imprisoned, mocked and insulted. The next morning he is placed before temple leaders and asked to tell them he is the Messiah. He responded, "If I tell you, you won't believe me. If I ask you, you would not answer. But from now on, the Son of Man will be seated at the right hand of God. Then they challenged, "Are you saying you are the Son of God?" Jesus responds, "You say that I am." They consider his response enough to convict him.

BETRAYED & EMOTIONALLY BRUISED
When I was a little girl, I acted out for attention and in all honesty, had a poor attitude. Often, I was accused of things or held responsible for things I didn't do. I grew used to it and developed a callous exterior. By the time I was a freshman, truth be told, I wasn't a virgin. But, I wasn't promiscuous either. I was curious enough to grant my virginity to a young man I thought loved me. I only had sex one time (not counting molestation).

Later that year, I attended my Freshman prom. My aunt really blessed us! She did my and two of my best friends hair and makeup. She escorted us to the prom. I had a beautiful dress that was white satin and lace. Upon arrival, several of the young men let me know I was beautiful. I felt like Cinderella on her magical evening. I never dance but felt so wonderful that a young man and I danced the night away.

At the time, my mom was dating a guy that despised me. He was good friends with another young ladies mother whose daughter, (who also hated me) told him I had sex with the boy I danced with all night. Even though my friends and I were chaperoned all night by my aunt and later went to IHOP with her, my mom believed her boyfriend. She accused me, refused to believe me and called me a slut.

I never had sex with that boy and I definitely didn't even talk to him off the dance floor. It made a wonderful memory bittersweet. My mother never even asked my aunt how it went, where we went or if I had fun. She just assumed the rumor was true. Which hurt me greatly.

"Persecuted, but not forsaken. Struck down, but not destroyed."
2 Corinthians 4:8

In Context

We walk in obedience and refuse to turn back because times are hard. We refuse to wear masks and play games. Everything we do and say is in the open, the truth on display, that people may judge us in the presence of God.

If our message isn't hitting the spot it's not due to lack of effort. Disinterest, refusal, or outright worship of things ungodly make a God-given message unattractive and seemingly useless.

The message is about and from Jesus, not his servants. We merely serve as a conduit through which the message arrives. If you merely see us, you will miss the beauty and overwhelming power of God that uses us to send the message.

We've been surrounded and battered by troubles. We aren't completely broken. We may not know what to do, but we trust God. Our faith may be tested, but God is right here. What they did to Jesus, they do to us. We are the hands and feet of Jesus, reflecting his will and his works. This is a real fight, our cross to bear. While we're going through the worst, you're getting in on the best.

We believe and speak truth that grace may abound, lives will be saved and God will be praised. While it looks like a pitiful mess on the outside, inwardly we are becoming spiritual warriors communing with God at higher levels and growing in faith. This is not the end, merely the beginning and it only gets better. What we see is smoke and mirrors yet what remains is truth and life - abundant and everlasting.

Final Notes

Our greatest regret would be to deny God's will for our lives. God's plan for our lives as his servants may not be outwardly glamorous, but they do guarantee us a seat at the table. There are days we will appear defeated but will actually be growing exponentially. Days of tears and pain in exchange for eternal glory. Don't look at your present situation or experience as torture, embrace the moment for this a day that God has tested your faith, strengthened your resolve and promoted you to conquer higher planes. Smoke and mirrors present shallow, microwavable, jiffy pop snacks that tide you over but never fill. Truth requires investigative, slow-cooking, patience and appreciation offering a far healthier and heartier meal that blesses you for eternity. It's your choice, pray that you will not fall into temptation as you walk, drawing your sword to fight a battle that's already been won.

Prayer

Lord Jesus, you know everything about us. From the crown of our heads to the soles of our feet, from our rising to our setting, from our flesh to the marrow within our bones. We are nothing, purely conduits of your love and message. Lord, our hearts are breaking as we suffer to serve in the way you ask. Help us to feel your presence, to cast our care, to trust and believe in spite of circumstance. Lord, bless us to move forward in confidence that we will reap, if we faint not. We believe we will see your goodness in the land of the living, our tents are camped in hope as we praise your Holy Name. You are our rock, our shield and our exceeding great reward. In you we have faith, in you we have hope, in you we believe. We pray for those that despitefully use us and condemn those that speak evil of us. No weapon formed against us shall prosper. Forgive us of our sins and help us to be all that you have created us to be.

In Jesus Name, Amen.

Loneliness

"Turn to me and be gracious to me, for I am lonely and afflicted."
Psalm 25:16

In Context

David confesses that his soul and trust belong to the Lord. He pleads that his enemies are unable to conquer him; for shame to rest on those who sin without shame but not on those who honor God; and for God to direct his path.

David prays for mercy and grace for past and present poor decisions; he reminds God of his goodness and his promise to teach sinners. That he promises guidance, goodness and mercy to those that respect the law of God: the meek.

He then asks for forgiveness. He further asserts that a man that fears the Lord, is blessed with the secret knowledge of God; that he is safe from danger and will rest while patiently awaiting deliverance.

David admits that his pain is great, that he is lonely and fearful that his enemies may triumph. He begs God to forgive him and to look upon the many that hate him and wish evil on him. He confesses his trust and vows to a commitment of integrity, patience and trust. He closes with a simple plea, "Save us."

ENEMIES AROUND EVERY CORNER

When I was in high school, there were three young ladies: two sisters and their cousin. They all purchased the same type of puffy jacket to wear (a trend at the time) and talked about people all the time.

Well on this day, they upset me and I told someone (not even sure who), that their jackets were getting scuffed and worn, resembling the bottom of an old swimming suit tattered and frayed from the cement of the pool surface. The person laughed and I thought nothing of it.

Later that day, the three girls approached me in the hallway. They were mad and one of them accused me of talking about her at the bus stop. I, being the sharp-minded idiot I was, looked at her and said, "Actually, I talked about you, your sister and your cousin," making sure to look at each one as I made reference to them. She was enraged. She lunged at me. I chose to focus solely on her as the other two joined in to fight me as well. Finally, after what seemed to be an eternity, a teacher broke up the fight. I'd adequately damaged the young ladies face that was their spokesperson and everyone knew not to mess with me... but in the end I felt betrayed by the young lady I'd told that to in confidence. Also, the young ladies I fought and I had been friends for years, I shouldn't have talked about them.

After being suspended and living across the street from each other we rekindled our friendship and she confided that it was indeed the young lady I'd told it to that began the drama. The next week we sat outside her house waiting on her to check the mail and kicked her butt. I was young and dumb.

The people that often betray us make dumb mistakes. Sometimes they are cold, calculated and intentional making us feel lonely, hated and in need of a Savior that understands the situation. If we trust God, we won't have to fight back or get revenge, we can leave that to him.

"Dearly beloved, avenge not yourselves, but rather give place unto wrath: for it is written, Vengeance is mine; I will repay, saith the Lord."
Romans 12:19

In Context
We are living sacrifices unto God. It's not too much of him to ask. We are to think differently, focusing only on the goodness of

God. We are called to be even-minded and less egotistical, God has distributed faith evenly among us all.

In fact, we all play important parts in God's divine plan and must work together. We each bring a unique gift to the table. Whether that's ministry or giving we are called to love and hate evil. To work together with kindness and to work hard, serving the Lord.

We are to hope, have patience, stay in prayer and bless those that despitefully use us. We are to bless and not curse. We are to allow God to get justice on our behalf as we instead be the hands and feet of Christ by loving, giving, blessing and serving those that hate us. In doing so, we overcome evil with good.

Final Notes
Instead of allowing our persecution to make us bitter, we are called to become better. We are living sacrifices unto God. It's not too much of him to ask as it was and is his greatest gift to us. Life in this manner can feel overwhelming, lonely and at times, fearful. Our enemies are strong, resilient, intentional and great in number. The blessing is that God promised us the victory if we just wait and allow him to work it out. Our responsibility is to be sober-minded and balanced, recognizing that God is no respecter of persons. We are the salt of the earth and anyone from the outside looking in should be able to recognize us as ambassadors of Christ.

Prayer

Most Gracious and Heavenly Father, we thank you for your loving arms of grace, love, mercy and truth. We confess that we are beyond blessed and that our circumstance has no power when faced with the almighty Word of God, the Spirit of truth and the blood of Jesus. We will honor, serve and represent you bringing our gifts, our love, our mercy and our forgiveness to the table. Lord, we humbly ask for your presence to be recognized and powerfully healing as we recover from broken hearts in the desolate, lonely and somewhat painful imprisonments of our minds. Forgive us, free us, heal us, save us Lord. We promise to obey, to trust and to love, which is our reasonable service.
In Jesus Name, Amen.

DAY
8

Unhealthy

"And a woman having an issue of blood twelve years, which had spent all her living upon physicians, neither could be healed of any, came behind him, and touched the border of his garment: and immediately her issue of blood stanched."
Luke 8:43-44

In Context

Jesus is teaching and healing as he goes from town to town with his disciples and a small group of women. Many were financing his travels while others were healed.

Jesus often spoke in parables (stories) to crowds but would speak directly to his disciples. He shared a story about the success of a seed. A seed goes into the ground, but its condition determines its fate. It will either: fall to the way side and be destroyed; land in the wrong area and whither; grow next to something that chokes it; or fall on good ground and grow to flourish with fruit. He then explained to his disciples that the seed in fact represented the Word of God. While explaining this, his mother and brother stood outside requesting his presence. Jesus in turn responds that those who hear the Word of God and do it are his family.

After these things, Jesus and his disciples travel to the other side of the lake. As they crossed, Jesus fell asleep but a fierce storm arose. The waves were so tumultuous they entered the large boat and the disciples feared for their lives. They awoke Jesus, saying, "Master, we perish." Jesus arose, asking "Where is your faith?" He revoked the sea and it calmed immediately. His disciples marveled at this.

They arrive on the other side to find a naked homeless man possessed by demons. Immediately the man cries,"What have I do to do with thee Jesus, Son of God? I beseech thee, torment me not." When asked his name, he responds, "We are legion." The demons within the man begged not to be destroyed but instead thrown into a herd of pigs. Jesus permitted it to be. As soon as the transfer was made, the entire herd of pigs fled off the cliff and were choked in the water. When witnesses reported to the town what happened and seeing the man filled with demons healed, they were very afraid of Jesus. They asked him to leave. The healed man begged to go but Jesus insisted he share his story with his neighbors. Then Jesus entered his boat and left.

When Jesus came back, every person was glad to see him. He was approached by a well respected leader with a 12-year old sick daughter. Jesus agreed to come heal the child and followed the man to his home. While en route, a woman sick for 12-years with an issue of blood, gently pushed through the crowd to touch the hem of Jesus garment. She did and was healed. Jesus felt healing power leave him and asked who touched him. Her faith gave her what doctors couldn't, it made her whole. Jesus told her to be of good comfort and to have peace. In the interim, the leader was told his daughter passed away. But Jesus insisted she was merely sleeping and continued to their home. They laughed, knowing she was dead. When they arrived Jesus made everyone leave, then took the young lady by the hand and said, "Maid, arise." She raised up and Jesus told her parents to feed her. Her parents were shocked, but Jesus told them not to tell anyone what happened.

HEALING THE BROKENHEARTED
Often times, we are placed on situations where pain is not only prevalent it is relevant. There are seasons when it seems everyone is going through, but with sunshine there must be rain, this is how we grow.

I was working hard, doing all that God commanded me to do. I loved my job and the work. I loved my purpose and the opportunities and ways in which to do it. I loved my life.

Then rain. Pain. Heartbreak. Depression. Suicidal thoughts... In that order. I began to reflect and that reflection began to echo and magnify until it was so loud that I could not hear God, all I could hear was pain, failure and the inability to correct. My heart was broken... shattered and those I thought I needed were no where to be found. I was sick.

Every year I create vision boards. For the past 4 years, I have continued to achieve and believe for everything not on this years board but also the boards of the past. They all looked at me as I looked at them. Last years board was made up of 90% scripture. They were daily affirmations. The only two cut out statements placed on the board were "The Personal Touch" and a "Good Idea in One City is a Good idea in all cities". Of all the books, classes and clients I served, those two statements were the most important to God. For clarification, this year, I published 'Obey: Obedience Breaks Every Yoke: Nothing is Bigger Than Our God', successfully managed and won my first political race with 73% of the vote, began selling my books on my own platform: MooreToRead.com, sent coloring books and art supplies to the Congo and took both my teen leadership classes out of market (Tulsa and Atlanta) successfully.

But what I found most important to God was healing. "The Personal Touch" is what I am experiencing as I write. After the election in November, I fell into a deep depression. I stopped working and lost several opportunities to succeed because I couldn't focus. The echoes of failure were loud and drowning out the promises of God. I couldn't move. I looked up at this board and realized this rain drop was part of God's magnificent plan to push me higher and to water my growth. Whenever I would read aloud this statement, I would alter it to say, "I will touch and clutch the gem of his garment to be made whole."

As 2016 began to close, artists and actors (public icons) were dying left and right. Prince, George Michael, Carrie Fisher, Debbie Reynolds.... God was using their story as a parable that he is destroying everything we think makes life more beautiful that we may see what actually make life wonderful - a relationship with him. My yoke is destroyed. My past is appreciated. My today with God cherished. My future shines bright. I am healed and healing. I am restored.

"Let your light so shine before men that they glorify your father in heaven for your good works." Matthew 5:16

In Context

Often referred to as "The Beatitudes," Matthew 5 shares great truth and understanding about the blessing of God. That even though we face tough times, we are in good company and recognized in heaven. That we are beacons of light, recognized by many and placed high to provide God's light and truth. The clarification being made by God as one that teaches lawlessness by action and one that teaches lawfulness in deed. The latter shall be called great and the former considered least in the kingdom of God. Anger without cause, resentment and verbal abuse are all considered murder in the eyes of God. Before we honor God with gift or sacrifice we must repent and forgive our fellow man and remit what is due when we can. Lust, swearing and revenge must rest behind us and we must mature by committing to do well, speak honestly and turn the other cheek. Pray for those that despitefully use you, for God rains on the just and unjust.

Final Notes

Pain will come, but we must recognize it is all a part of God's strategic plan to help us become what he has created us to be. It is not all good, but will work together for the good. We cannot avenge, but instead forgive. We must allow God to do his healing work in us, leaving our emotional wounds behind and embracing the wonderful future that lies before us with two hands. If one hand is still holding our baggage from the wilderness, we are going to miss our blessing. If half of our heart is broken with pain, we have nothing to give the person we were sent to heal. We have to just let go and let God heal us and correct the wrongs. We are strong, we are delivered and we are healed!

Prayer

Lord, we are so blessed! Thank you for healing us. Thank you for correcting us. Thank you for saving us. As we continue on this journey, comfort us in times of pain or great sorrow. Quiet the loud and thundering threats of defeat that surround us, restore our faith and trust in you, direct our path and make it straight. Grant us wisdom and discernment to make choices that are pleasing in your sight and forgive us of our sins as we forgive those that have hurt us. Impart supernatural strategies that bless those you have sent us to serve, open doors of promotion and abundance, do exceedingly more than we can ask, think or imagine. We give you all the praise, all of the honor and the glory.

In Jesus Name, Amen.

Into the Promised Land

DAY
9

Poor, Angry and Making Bad Choices

"Now there was a famine in the land; so Abram went down to Egypt to sojourn there, for the famine was severe in the land. It came about when he came near to Egypt, that he said to Sarai his wife, "See now, I know that you are a beautiful woman; and when the Egyptians see you, they will say, 'This is his wife'; and they will kill me, but they will let you live. "Please say that you are my sister so that it may go well with me because of you, and that I may live on account of you."
Genesis 12: 10-13

In Context

God told Abram to travel to a land he would show him. As he traveled, God promised Abram he and his family would bless nations to come. He also promised him that the land he was walking on (Canaan) would belong to his descendants. Abram built a memorial on honor of God's promise. Famine forced Sarai and Abram to enter Egypt where Abram feared for his life because of Sarai's beauty. He asked her to tell them they were siblings instead of husband and wife.

The Egyptians saw her and admonished her beauty before Pharaoh who quickly summoned her. She and Abram were treated well. But God plagued Pharaoh's house and gave him nightmares. He awakened and summoned Abram, asking, "Why didn't you tell me she was your wife?" He told them to leave and allowed them to take all of their belongings.

POOR AND MAKING BAD CHOICES

God has made several promises to me in life. I remember packing up and leaving Atlanta with my two daughters under the belief in a promise.

We moved to Fairfax, Va. I had some 401k money, no job and we were living in an Extended Stay hotel. I was poor and angry.

Is this what the promise looked like? I was obedient, responding to every direction God gave... so why was life like this?

As money dwindled, we were rejected for state services, no one was hiring a young lady with my skill set and life was going from bad to worse.

I was down to six dollars in change. I used it to go to a job interview. After, interviewing up the chain and 6 hours later, I began to head home. I ran out of gas (which I knew was possible but refused to miss the interview), t-mobile had just cut my phone off and I was stuck.

I looked at the prayer ministry cards that spoke of God's faithfulness and allowed them to encourage me. Even though I hadn't gotten one call for the prayer line, I still believed the promises, "He knows, He lives, He cares."

I got out and began walking. I was not even ten steps away from my car before a man offered help. He went to the gas station and got enough gas to get me back on the road, had me follow him to the gas station to get more gas, then gave me directions home.

I didn't get the job. I was poor, angry (at God) and making poor choices. Eventually, I had to come home to Oklahoma... within a year, I'd been hired at a local television station that promoted me to Marketing Coordinator. The promise was fulfilled.

"But the men that went up with him said, We be not able to go up against the people; for they are stronger than we." Numbers 13:31

In Context

God instructed Moses to send one man from each tribe into Canaan, the land he promised them, to spy it out. He also sent the son of Nun Jehoshua. He instructed, "Go and see the land and the people that dwelleth there, whether they are strong or weak, few or many; And what their land is they dwell in, whether it be good or bad; and what cities they be that they dwell in, whether in tents, or in strong holds; And what the land is, whether it be fat or lean, whether there be wood therein, or not. And finally, be of good courage, and bring of the fruit of the land."

They left, and searched from Zin to Rehob, from Hamath to Hebron (where the children of Anak lived), then to the brook of Eshcol where they cut down a large cluster of grapes (two people forced to carry), figs and pomegranates. They returned to report their findings after 40 days.

Fruit in hand, they approached and reported,"The land does flow with milk and honey, and this is the fruit but, the people are too strong for us, the city is fortified with large walls, and the children of Anak reside there."

But Caleb was positive they could take the land. The others instead again resisted believing that it was too difficult, referring to themselves as grasshoppers in the land.

Final Notes

Fear will keep us from pursuing God's best. It will allow us to settle for mediocrity when God promised to protect, provide and direct us. We are called to stay in faith and believe God.

Prayer

Lord, as we face our Jordan Rivers gushing with reasons not to believe, strengthen our faith. Help us to confess your word in prayer and to pray without ceasing. Help us to hear your voice and strictly follow your command. Help us to obey your will when our situation tries to tell us not to. You have not given us a spirit of fear, but of love and a sound mind. We honor you, we glorify you and we praise you!

In Jesus Name, Amen.

DAY
10

God Heals

"God heals the broken-hearted and binds up there wounds."
Psalm 147:3

In Context

Give God the praise! Praise is beautiful. God builds Jerusalem and gathers the outcasts. He heals the broken-hearted and binds their wounds. He knows every star. The Lord is great. He is all powerful and his wisdom is unsearchable. He lifts the meek and casts down the wicked. Thank God and sing songs of praise with harps. Praise he who makes rain, grass, food for the beast and who hears the raven cry. He has no delight in those that have the strength of a horse, or strong legs but instead those that fear him and hope in his mercy. Praise the Lord! He has fortified your city, he has blessed your children, he has surrounded you with peace and given you wheat. He sends his commands on earth and his Word runs swiftly. He gives snow as wool, frost as ashes, ice as morsels... who can stand before his Word? He sends his Word and it all melts, waters flow and winds blow. His Word he shares with Jacob, statutes and judgments to Israel. He has not dealt this way with any nation and as for his judgments, they have not known them. Praise ye the Lord.

HEALED AND DELIVERED

When I was 29 I moved to Atlanta. I'd been a recent victim of a violent acquaintance rape (someone I met online) and I needed to get out of my house and to a safe space. I left a great job with a company I truly loved and began an adventure in Georgia.

It was difficult being a single mother and providing for my family where the cost of living wasn't extreme but compared to my pay... it was tight. I was trying hard to fit in. A group of my peers (friends I'd made and began to trust) introduced me to ecstasy. A coworker introduced me to coke. I fell hard and fast. I knew I was in way too deep and I turned to God for help. I didn't really know God but I knew I needed help.

I began to read the Bible and pray. I started matching my tithe to the amount I spent on drugs each week, slipping it beneath the door of the church after I thought or believed service was over. One day, a man caught me dropping off my offering. He asked, "If you died today, would you know you were going to heaven?"

I had to say no. I was still doing coke and my habit had control. He invited me to get baptized. On the day of my baptismal I was high, the minister knew and hesitated but The Holy Spirit must have whispered in his ear because he took me down in that water. My children and husband (have to explain how he ended up back in the picture later) watched.

From that day forward (really before then when I started reading the Bible) I knew that God was with me and loved me. I was at my worst and he loved me. He healed me too. I have been clean 8 years and never visited a rehab. Instead, when I failed I would pray, "Your grace is sufficient for in my weakness is your strength made perfect." and when I stopped but wanted to do drugs, I prayed, " Get thee behind me Satan."

"And she said, Truth, Lord: yet the dogs eat of the crumbs which fall from their masters' table." Matthew 15:27

In Context
The leaders of the temple asked Jesus why his disciples didn't wash their hands before eating, accusing them of breaking tradition. Jesus responded with his own question: "Why do you not honor the tradition of God?" Referencing their allowance of dishonor toward their mothers and fathers to be dismissed with gift giving. He added,

the people draw nigh with their lips but their hearts are far from me. They teach in vain. It is not what goes in a mans mouth that defiles them but what comes out of a mans mouth. His disciples told him the religious teachers were upset by his remarks. He responded that Every plant God hasn't planted will be plucked up. They are the blind leading the blind and that they will all fall into the ditch. This confused Peter and he asked for clarification.

Jesus asked, "Do you not understand?" He then clarified, what we process through our mouths enters the belly and later becomes waste. But what we say comes from the heart and defiles a man. From the heart we develop evil thoughts, murder, adultery, fornication, theft and false witness... these are the things which defile a man, eating with unclean hands does not.

Then he traveled to the coasts of Tyre where he was approached by a Canaanite woman whose daughter was possessed by demons. She begged him to help her but Jesus remained silent and his disciples asked to send her away. Then Jesus replied, "I am sent to serve the lost sheep of Israel." But she worshipped him and pleaded for his help. He then replied, "It is not fair to take the children's bread and cast it to dogs." She replied, "Truth. But the dogs eat the crumbs that fall from the masters table." Jesus was impressed. He said, "Woman, great is thy faith. You will get what you desire." Her daughter was healed within the hour.

Then Jesus traveled the Sea of Galilee and went up into a mountain. Many brought their sick: lame, blind, maimed and others and he healed them. They gave God the glory. Three days passed. Jesus called his disciples, he wanted to give them something to eat. He asked if anyone had food. They told him they had seven loaves of bread and a few little fishes. He took them, gave thanks, broke them and told the disciples to distribute them. Every person ate and afterward what was leftover filled seven baskets. Four thousand were fed. After Jesus traveled by ship to Magdala.

Final Notes

God sees us. He knows what has broken our hearts and why we are where we are. He knows the good, the bad and the ugly. If you are meek, he will lift you up. If you are undeserving, he will grant you your desires when you worship and acknowledge your truth. God is a gracious and loving God. He will heal us in our broken place. Praise him, lift him on high. He is worthy to be praised! What we say and believe is what leaves our hearts but we must be careful it is not for show. God knows the inner workings of our hearts. He knows us. We can Google His Word but not his wisdom.

Prayer

Lord Jesus, forgive us of our sins and please heal our land. Restore our peace and rebuild our fortified cities. Replenish our wheat and help us to worship you in wholeness and in truth. We will not be stingy with our praise, we will honor you with our hearts and our hands before transgressing with our lips. Help us not to judge but to be your vessels of light, love and mercy. Teach us your will and grant us the wisdom to walk it out. We love you. We thank you. We bless your holy and righteous name.

In Jesus Name, Amen.

DAY
11

Forgiveness

"Who is a God like you, who pardons sin and forgives the transgression of the remnant of his inheritance? You do not stay angry forever but delight to show mercy." Micah 7:18

In Context

God addresses idol worship and sin; disregard for the blessings and gifts of righteousness he has shown his people in Micah 6. In Micah 7, he talks about repentance and restoration by a merciful God. He begins by addressing the current state of desolation and desire... that they have become blood thirsty, ruthless and driven by success. He says it is so bad that they cannot trust a friend, a guide, a girlfriend or the members of their household. Then the writer says, "But I will wait on my Lord..." The Lord of his salvation and who will hear him. He warns his enemies not to rejoice because when he falls, he will rise, when it is dark, God will be his light and reflect his righteousness. Then his enemy will see and be ashamed... trodden in the streets. Then the curse will be lifted, God will come through the fortified city (over sea and above mountains) to a desolate land to feed them and show them marvelous things. The nations will watch in shock and bewilderment as they try to close their mouths and shut their eyes. It will be too late, like a snake they will slither the ground in shame and fear God because of your recovery. "Who is a God like you? Who forgives sin and doesn't stay angry forever but delights in mercy?" God will forgive us, have compassion on us, and throw our sins into the sea of forgetfulness. You will perform truth to Jacob and mercy to Abraham our fathers of old.

HE DELIGHTS IN MERCY

When I lived in Atlanta, I totaled 6 cars in one year. Not because I was high behind the wheel, but because I was constantly financially and emotionally overwhelmed. I suffered from anxiety. I was a distracted driver.

After a stressful day at work, during wall to wall traffic, on a day I was to meet family to watch my brother perform... I had an accident, my 4th of the year. The red light before, I remember recognizing I was distracted and saying out loud to myself, "If I keep this up, I am going to have an accident."

Sure enough, one traffic light later, I looked to see a yellow light, decided to cruise through, looked down to change the radio or grab my phone... and looked up to find myself about to t-bone a young lady in the car in front of me.

I quickly lifted both hands up and clasped them together in prayer position, and said, "God, please don't let me kill this woman." I hit the brakes as hard as I could but it was obviously too late. The force of the impact was so bad that as my air bag deployed, it cracked the bone in my pinky finger (that was in prayer position). The air bag also cracked my windshield. My leg was pinned between the car door and the front left area of the car. I was dazed and confused, sitting in the intersection. When I gathered myself, I looked up at two older white women staring at me from their car. I asked them what happened and one of them mouthed, "You ran the red light." I believed her.

I was able to free my leg and walked over to ask the woman in her car if she was ok. She said that her back hurt but other than that she was ok. I didn't kill her or break her in half... I was so thankful! The police arrived. I remember looking at the back of my insurance card which read, "Never admit guilt." I thought, "Whatever."

I told that policemen everything. He looked at me and said, "No one ever tells the truth in these accidents. They always blame the other person." I knew I was beyond blessed and could have killed that young lady and that is something I never would have been able to stomach. I was not charged and free to go. As I write this I imagine what could have happened. I prayed and God heard me. It could have ended with me behind bars but God delighted in forgiveness and mercy that day, and his delight is truly my joy. I am so grateful to have a God that sits high and looks low and shows mercy on his people.

"Though the LORD be high, yet hath he respect unto the lowly: but the proud he knoweth afar off." Psalm 138:6

In Context

Psalm 138 says, "I will praise thee with my WHOLE heart! I will sing praises before all because you value you your promise above your name. When I cried to you, you strengthened me within my soul. Every king shall worship you when they hear your truth. They will sing the ways of the Lord, for great is the glory of the Lord. The the Lord sit high, he has respect for the lowly and keeps distant from the proud. Though I am in trouble, you will restore me and avenge my enemies... your right hand shall save me. The Lord will perfect that which concerns me and his mercy endures forever. Forsake not the work of the hands oh Lord.

Final Notes

We will require a lifetime of God's mercy. No one is exempt. God is not only faithful to forgive, he will also show us mercy and put those that talked about us or attempted to harm us to shame. God says, he will break through our fortified cities crossing sea and climbing mountains to show us marvelous things. That is a reason to shout. God knew us before we made that mistake and he sees the end from the beginning.

Prayer

Lord Jesus! Thank you, thank you, thank you for loving me in spite of me. We have all fallen short of your glory and we are so grateful that you delight in showing us mercy. Help us to rebuild. Help us to restore. Help us to forgive those that have wronged us. Help us to show your love and mercy toward others. Thank you for blessing us and thank you for keeping us. Please grant us wisdom and discernment to make choices that are pleasing in your sight.
In Jesus Name, Amen.

Into the Promised Land

DAY
12

Loveliness

"How lovely is your dwelling place, LORD Almighty!" Psalm 84:1

In Context

How wonderful it is to spend time with God! My soul cries out for you. Even the birds find a home, but those that dwell with you will still be praising you. Blessed is the man whose strength is in thee. They go from strength to strength, every one in Zion appears before God. God is our shield. Look at the face of the anointed. A day in the courts is a thousand and I would rather be a doorkeeper in the house of God than dwell with the wicked. No good thing will God uphold from those that walk uprightly. Blessed is the man that trusts in you.

BLESSED & TRUSTING GOD

It was election day. Everything bad that could happen did. The candidate was sick, I was overworked and tired, our opponent beat us to the door the night before and we didn't have enough walkers. The candidate was irritated, tired and losing hope.

But I had faith.

We'd done everything we knew how to do. We had a great phone bank, excellent robo calls, consistent communication with the voter, great commercials, wonderful mail outs, yard signs in prominent influential locations and a candidate that wasn't afraid of hard work.

And faith.

God had been speaking to me about the campaign from the beginning. He'd told me when and how to operate, to stick with it and to have faith, we were going to win. Even when it got tough at the finish line, I never stopped believing. Politics can get ugly. If you aren't the type to get ugly people look at it as a weakness, but they are wrong. It is a strength when you know that your character, hard work and faith will see you through.

It was time to see who won. We'd called every voter we could and even sent one last robo call... we were at the finish line. The first location was our base and we only won by 8 votes. I felt a shiver of doubt creep up my spine but I refused to acknowledge possible defeat. We went to the next location, we lost by 6 votes. Only ahead by two votes made the trip to the next location all the more tense. Finally, ahead by 21 votes. On to the next, ahead by 50. Friends began to text and let us know we did great with absentee and early voting. This was it, we won. While there were 6 more precincts, we knew at that point, we'd beat them. These were the largest and highest voting areas in our district. Afterward, I kept seeing the word faith. I knew God was pleased with my faith.

"Finally, brethren, whatsoever things are true, whatsoever things are honest, whatsoever things are just, whatsoever things are pure, whatsoever things are lovely, whatsoever things are of good report; if there be any virtue, and if there be any praise, think on these things." Phillipians 4:8

In Context

Dearly beloved and longed for, my joy and my crown, be strong in the Lord. Paul prays that the areas he served unite in their thinking and care for those that helped him spread the gospel. Rejoice! The Lord is with us. Don't worry, pray. Thank God, tell him what you need and the peace of God will develop around you and in your heart through Christ Jesus. Focus on what is true, honest, just, pure, lovely and of good report. If it has virtue and praise, think about this. I am glad your care for me has continued, for a while you weren't able. I have learned to be content wherever I am: hungry or fed. I can do all things through Christ who strengthens me. Thank you for recognizing my affliction. You were the only church that financially supported my ministry from the beginning. I don't share this because I desire a gift but because you deserve fruit they may increase. I have increased thanks to your gift, a great and pleasing gift in God's eyes. God will supply all your needs according to his riches and glory in Christ Jesus. Give God the glory and salute your brothers and sisters in Christ. The grace of our Lord be with you, Amen.

Final Notes

We all suffer at times. We must endure and look at these times as God strengthening us for the battle ahead. We must train our hearts to beat in accordance to Gods will, knowing he sees us. Pray, thank God, tell him what you need, receive his peace then think about the best in life. Focus on the good. Don't let your current situation cause you to become bitter and broken. You have the power to change how you see it. Think lovely.

Prayer

Lord, you are strong and mighty in battle. We are tired and weak. We cast our care on you. We thank you for every blessing of mercy, grace and abundance. We praise you for our current circumstance by your design. We praise you for our testing and trial for in the end we will prove your presence was with us. Help us. Remove the bitter root of discontent, discouragement, defeat and betrayal. Replace it with love, patience, comfort and support. Our minds are scattered with nightmares of what could be, replace those images with those of victory, success and triumph. We can't survive this without you. Hide us from the darts of our enemies, avenge us oh Lord. We can't breathe without your help.

In Jesus Name, Amen.

This Was Ordained

"For if thou altogether holdest thy peace at this time, then shall there enlargement and deliverance arise to the Jews from another place; but thou and thy father's house shall be destroyed: and who knoweth whether thou art come to the kingdom for such a time as this?"
Esther 4:14

In Context

Mordecai was mortified by the actions of Haman to destroy the Jews. He laid in front of the kings gate in trodden clothing and among the ashes. He sent word to his niece Esther about what was happening and requested she defend her people before the king. Esther knew approaching the king without permission was punishable by death. She feared taking this step. She sent her message to Mordecai along with clothing and asked him to clean up and rise. He refused. He sent a message back sharing that she ought not believe she will be spared when destruction comes because it will reach her and her fathers house. That instead she should consider her promotion was ordained for this moment of influence. She replied that she would fast along with her maidens without food or water for three days and asked that he and all the Jews do so as well. After three days, she would approach the king and if she perished, she perished.

Take Me to the King

Are you blessed to be a blessing but holding back to save yourself? This is the question I have asked myself so many times over the years when choosing between what God asked me to do and what makes common sense.

I was in a season where everything was winding down. I was almost done with the campaign work, just held two successful classes for teen girls, finished my fourth book: Obey and was resting on a nice cruise. My money was funny and my change was strange but I kept feeling the press of God that now was the time to promote my young men's class. But I was hesitant. I knew I couldn't afford it. But I kept feeling the press of God. So I did it. The class filled in less than a week with standing room only! It was awesome. Finally it was time to award the winner his laptop but I didn't have the funds. Thank God I was good friends with his mother and they were patient because little did I know, I was in for the most barren season of my adult life.

First, my campaign work ended - abruptly but necessarily. Second my bills were due. First my phone, then the water, then the Internet and my rent. My family and friends turned their backs on us. My kids and I spent the holidays alone, suffering. But God. I reached out to a former client for work. She hired me to do her website. Ok cool. Then she lost an employee and asked could I cover as they transitioned shifts, sure - I had time and there were backend items needed that I could work on while there. The day I reported to start helping out my electric was shut off. I cried most of the morning but hustled to get projected projects done. As I worked on a product line for her, she came back and told me God wanted her to help me. I had no idea what she was talking about but she proceeded to write me an $800 check. I praised God because I never said a word to her about my need. So fast forward. It's the beginning of the year and we survived the holidays. God called me to a place of strict obedience and I did all he asked. When my landlord called, I prayed God help me to be honest and strong. Next thing you know my landlord waived my late rent. Then he stopped by to make sure my utilities were on. My water had been cut off for four weeks at that point. He PAID my $400 water bill and told me that by now we knew each other and he has my back. You never know who is paying attention to you but keep going!!! The day prior and that day two clients paid invoices and one was featured on the local news! God will send angels to bless you in the nick of time! Run your race and keep doing whatever he says! This situation has been ordained.

"And Joseph was a goodly person, and well favoured. And it came to pass after these things, that his master's wife cast her eyes upon Joseph; and she said, Lie with me. But he refused, and said unto his master's wife, Behold, my master wotteth not what is with me in the house, and he hath committed all that he hath to my hand;" Genesis 39:6-8

In Context

Joseph was a slave brought to work in an Egyptian home owned by a man named Potiphar. Joseph was blessed. Potiphar trusted Joseph. It was obvious to him that God's hand was all over his life. He knew that he was blessed in his home and field because Joseph was in his life and he withheld nothing from him. Joseph was a good and honorable servant and steward. One day his wife lusted for Joseph but he refused her. Day by Day she continued her advancements, but Joseph honored his commitment to Potiphar and more importantly to God. But one day he went inside the home where he was alone and she trapped him. She snatched the clothes off his back as he ran from her. Then she cried attempted rape. When Potiphar got home and saw what happened he was angry. He threw Joseph in prison, but even in jail Joseph was blessed. The jailer trusted Joseph and made him overseer of all in the prison. He did not worry about his responsibilities because Joseph was taking care of it all.

Final Notes

What we are experiencing today is for God's glory. God's glory! If we had pleasant lives without battles that could be witnessed from afar, where would we be? This is why Mordecai refused to get up, this is why he challenged Esther. How could we continue in faith or encourage others without a battle for people to watch us win? Without proving we trust God? Our present season is a test for a testimony. God is blessing us and he will change our situation after a while. Stay strong, have faith and run until we see what the end will be.

Prayer

Dear Lord Jesus! You are an awesome God. Your grace and your mercy has carried us from valley to mountaintop, from ashes to gladness, from disobedience to obedience and from sin to cleansed. Thank you. Thank you for remaining consistent in a world of inconsistencies, for being faithful and loving in the midst of our storms. For blessing us in prison while we wait for the palace. For keeping your anointed hand on our lives and pushing us through. Help us to run. Help us to build fortified cities of wisdom, love, gratitude and praise. Forgive us of our sins and help us become all that you have called us to be!

In Jesus Name, Amen.

DAY
14

Light

"Then spake Jesus again unto them, saying, I am the light of the world: he that followeth me shall not walk in darkness, but shall have the light of life."
John 8:12

In Context

Jesus went to Mt. Olive. Early the next day Jesus went into the temple and taught. The scribes and Pharisees brought a woman caught in the act of adultery into the temple and through her before Jesus. They insisted the law required she be stoned. But they left it up to Jesus, trying to trick him. Rather than answer them Jesus bent down and with his finger wrote in the ground. They insisted he respond. Jesus finally answered, "He that is without sin, cast the first stone." All those that were around eventually left leaving Jesus and the woman alone. He arose and looked around to see everyone was gone he then asked her "Woman, where are your accusers? Has no one condemned thee?" She replied, "No man," and Jesus replied, "Neither do I, go and sin no more." Then Jesus addressed the crowd, "I am the light of the world, he that follows me shall not walk in darkness, but shall have the light of life." But the Pharisees accused him of being self-centered and a liar. "I am talking about me, but I am not lying. I know where I came from and where I am going. You don't know where I came from or where I am going," Jesus continued, "You are judging the flesh, but I don't judge anyone. But if I do judge, it's the truth because I am never alone, my father sent me. The law says, two witnesses confirm truth. I bear witness of myself and the father bears witness of me." The Pharisees asked, "Where is your father?" "Because you don't know me, you don't know my Father. If you had known me I wouldn't know you know my Father. I am going to go my own way and you will look for me but where I'm going you can't come and you will die in your sins." The Jews asked themselves if he was going to kill himself because he said where he's going they can't come. "You are from below and I am from above; you are of this world and I am not of this world. You are going to die in your sins because you don't believe that I am he and you are going to die in your sins." At this they asked, "Who are you?" Jesus replied, "The same that I said to you from the beginning I have many things to judge of you, but he that sent me is true and I speak to the world those things I have heard of him." The Jews were confused. "When you have lifted up the Son of Man then you will know that I am he and that I did with the Father told me and did not speak of myself. And that he that sent me is with me, my Father has not left me alone because I always do those things that please him." As he spoke this, many believed him. He spoke to those that believed, "If you are my disciples indeed then you will know the truth and the truth will set you free." The Jews responded, "We are the seed of Abraham and have never been any man's slave, how are you going to say that we are going to be free?"

"Whoever commits sin is the servant of sin and will not stay in the house but I shall abide in the house forever. If the sun shall make you free shall be free indeed. I know you are Abraham seed, but you seek to kill me - my word has no place in you. I speak that which I have seen with my Father and you do what you have seen with your father."

They replied, "Abraham is our father." "If that were true you would do the works of Abraham. You seek to kill me, A man that has told you the truth which I have heard of God, Abraham would not do this - you do the works of your father," Jesus answered. "We are not born of fornication, God is our Father," they answered. "If God were your Father, you would love me because I came from God, he sent me. Why can't you understand me? Why can't you hear me? Because your father is the devil, and the lusts of your father that is what you do. He was a murderer from the beginning and lived not in the truth because the truth is not in him. When he tells a lie it's a lie of his own because he is a liar and the father of lies. And I tell you the truth but you don't believe me. Which of you has convinced me of sin? If I say the truth, why do you not believe me? He that is of God, hears God's words, but if you don't hear them it's because your not of him." Then the Jews responded, "Didn't we have it right? He's a Samaritan and has a devil." Jesus answered, "I don't have a devil, I honor my father and you dishonor me. I seek not my own glory, there's one at seeks and judges. Verily, Verily I say unto you if a man keeps my saying, he will not see death."Then the Jews responded, "Now we know he has a devil. Abraham is dead and the prophets are dead but if we believe what he says, we will not see death? Are you greater than Abraham or the prophets who are dead? Who do you make yourself?" Jesus answered, "If I honor myself, my honor is nothing. It is my father that honors me, of whom you say that he is your God. You have not known him, but I know him, and if I should say that I don't know him, I would be a liar like you. But I know and obey him. Your father Abraham rejoiced to see my day, when he saw it, he was happy." They responded, "You aren't 50 years old and you have seen Abraham?" Then they picked up stones to throw at Jesus but Jesus disappeared amongst them and passed them by.

UNRECOGNIZABLE

We all love recognition! Especially when we have worked hard to become who we've become and defied every obstacle placed before us. But, despite our best efforts, there are days when we are simply, unrecognizable.

When I was little my grandfather was blind. He and my wonderful grandmother had 11 kids and close to 40 grandchildren, if not more. My grandfather could only see shadows.

One day, standing next to his brown leather easy chair, my grandfather grabbed my shoulders as my cousin Stacy stood next to me. "Stacy!" He said in his jovial welcoming way, that always made you smile. I said, "No grandfather, it's Stephanie!" I was heartbroken in a way but ok. My cousin and I had similar names and were close in height. But I wanted grandfather to know it was me!

Sometimes we get upset because people can't see the real you. They reject or make fun of us. But it's ok, because God looks at the heart and he knows EXACTLY who you are.

"But the LORD said to Samuel, "Do not consider his appearance or his height, for I have rejected him. The LORD does not look at the things people look at. People look at the outward appearance, but the LORD looks at the heart."
I Samuel 16:7

In Context
The Lord rejected Saul as king and told Samuel to stop mourning. He sent him a man named Jesse's house, where he promised a king amongst his sons. Samuel goes to Jesse's house to anoint the one God favors. He shares that he is there to give a sacrifice to God and he anoints Jesse and his sons with oil, sanctifying them for worship. When Samuel saw Jesse's son Eliab, he knew it must be him. But God said, don't look at his stature, height or his appearance. I don't see as man sees, I look at the heart. So every son was brought before Samuel without response from God. There were seven. Samuel asked Jesse, "Are these all of your sons?" He told him the youngest was tending sheep. Samuel had him call for him. The young man came in: small, dirty and ugly. The Lord said, "Anoint him. This is the one." That day the Spirit of the Lord came upon David and departed from Saul. An evil spirit from the Lord troubled him. His servants recognized it and asked to seek a man that could play a harp and ease his mind. They told him of a young man that was cunning and prudent, a warrior with the Spirit of God that could play the harp. He sent a message to Davids father requesting the son that tends the sheep. Jesse sent David, a bottle of wine, a kid and bread. Saul was pleased with David and made him his armor bearer. He sent a message to his father asking him to permit David to stay with him and he did, playing the harp for him when needed. The evil spirit departed from him.

Final Notes
Jesus is our Savior. While we may not look like the one God chose, God knows our hearts. Stay in faith. God will anoint and appoint

those whose hearts are in alignment with his. Stay strong, ignore opposition and keep moving forward in the work God has given you to do.

Prayer

Most Gracious and Heavenly Father, thank you. Your recognition is all that we need. You promise that if we honor you before men, we will be honored by men. Thank you for your unending love, mercy and grace. Thank you for blessing us and keeping us. Thank you for those that see you in us. Thank you for those that support us. You are our rock, our shield and our exceeding great reward. Forgive us where we fall short and strengthen us to keep going.

We love you.

In Jesus Name, Amen.

DAY 15

Speak Life

"Death and life are in the power of the tongue: and they that love it shall eat the fruit thereof." Proverbs 18:21

In Context

What you say has power. Loners that only care for themselves don't recognize goodness for all. Fools speak too much. Shame follows evil. Many words flow like a river but wisdom is a refreshing spring that flows upward. It's unjust to be good to the guilty or hard on the innocent. Fools say things that stir trouble and crush them, shut them up to save them. Listening to gossip will make you sick and laziness is destruction. God's name is a strong tower you can run to for safety. Rich people think their money is wall of protection. Pride goes before a mighty fall and humility before honor. It is unintelligent to answer before listening and rude as well. A healthy spirit conquers adversity and but what can you do when a spirit is crushed? Wisdom seeks and absorbs new lessons and insight. A gift gets attention, it buys the attention of powerful people. It all sounds good at first until it is closely inspected. Drawing straws may be the only answer to tough choices and do a favor to win a friend for life - nothing strips that bond. Words are as fulfilling and refreshing as fresh vegetation; and right words as great as harvest. Words can either kill or give life, it's your choice. A man that finds a wife, gains good life and finds favor with God. The poor speak softly, the rich bark like dogs. Friends come and they go, but a true friend sticks by you like family.

SPEAK LIFE

My daughter and I were speaking one evening as she proceeded to tell me her plans for the next weekend. She'd been doing odd jobs as a photographer to make money now and again but those instances were few and far between. She explained, "Next week my best friend and I are going to see this movie." I responded, "Really? You haven't received permission or even asked to go. Beyond that, you don't have any money." She smiled. "Mama, I was going to ask you next week. Closer to the day (side eye from me). Besides, I know I am going to have some money," she says confidently. "Oh really? You don't have a job! How do you expect to do that? I don't think you will have it next week," I reply. She twists her body to look me boldly in the face and says, "I am speaking it into existence!" All I could do was laugh, knowing I taught her this and we have seen God honor this truth so many times. That same evening, I am resting on the same couch, listening to E. Dewey Smith and I get a text from my brother in Atlanta. It reads, "Sent some money to your Paypal for Brooklyn. Let me know you got it." Sure enough, he'd sent her $25. I laughed because the first thing I heard was her saying, "I'm speaking it into existence." I knew God was trying to remind me of a very important principle. Our words have power. I told her that my brother sent that money and she was so surprised! I reminded her of what she said. She looked at me and said, "Yup!" Visibly proud of herself for believing in a law of God.

"O taste and see that the Lord is good: blessed is the man that trusteth in him."
Psalms 34:8

In Context

I will always confess that I love God and praise him! Even my soul will boast in God for he is good, the humble will hear and be happy. Won't you join me in praising the Lord? I sought God and he heard my prayer and delivered me from every fear. They that looked to God were lightened and without shame. Yes when I cried, God saved me! The angels of the Lord encircle his believers and deliver them. Taste and see that the Lord is good, and blessed is the man who trusts in him. Fear God, for there is no want to those that fear him. Those that seek the Lord lack nothing good! How do you fear God, speak love not hate, do good and not evil, hunt peace. The Lord is ever watching the righteous and listening for their cry. The evil will be destroyed but God will hear the righteous. God heals the broken hearted and down trodden in spirit. Many are the afflictions of the righteous but God saves from each one. He keeps all his bones and not one is broken. Evil shall slay the wicked and he that hates the righteous shall be desolate. The Lord redeems the souls of the righteous and none of them shall be desolate.

Final Notes

Our words can bring such beautiful life. Faith comes by hearing the Word of God. If only we taste, believe and stand on our faith by taking action will we be able to see the full promise of God. God adds that a person who marries finds favor with him in the middle of a chapter about how we speak. That means our words help us to build relationships that will rain favor on us for a lifetime! We can do this if we only believe. If we doubt God, our words will be full of bitterness, envy, strife and hatred. Instead, we must trust God and allow what is in our hearts to flow from our mouths. God IS Good.

Prayer

Lord Jesus, we are so thankful to you for blessing us. We are grateful to have your presence and your glory and your love. You are so awesome. God help us to be perfect conduits of your exponential blessing over our lives. Help us to increase in love, generosity, mercy and grace as we decrease in selfishness, gossip, foolishness and hate. Restore us to a place filled with your light that our shame may be hidden and our sins washed clean. We love you and thank you. Lay your hands of anointing power over us and fill us with supernatural wisdom and discernment to make choices that are pleasing in your sight. Help us to speak words that are containers of your creativity, genius and necessary invention to restore, rebuild and protect your children and their children that your name may reign forevermore. Forgive us of our sins and help us to be a blessing to someone else.

In Jesus Name, Amen.

Loving Myself

*"And the Lord shall make thee the head, and not the tail; and thou shalt
be above only, and thou shalt not be beneath; if that thou hearken unto the
commandments of the Lord thy God, which I command thee this day, to observe
and to do them:" Deuteronomy 28:13*

In Context

Blessings and the Curse

It will happen if you listen carefully to God and do everything he
instructs. He will set you high above nations. You will be blessed:

· In the city and field, everywhere you go
· To will produce fruit in your body, ground, and flocks.
· In Thy basket and they store
· When you come in and go out
· In Your stores and whatever you set your hand to
· In the Land the Lord Gives you

The Lord will make your enemies that rise against you come one way
but flee seven ways. He will make you a holy people if you promise
to walk in all his ways. And all the people will see that you walk with
God and fear you. The Lord will multiply your value, in the fruit of
your body, your harvest and your stock in your promised land. The
Lord will open the land of his good treasure, the rain in his season,
and bless the work you do that you may lend, not borrow, to many
across nations. And the Lord shall make you the head and not the
tail, above and not beneath, the lender and not the borrower - if -
you do as he commands. Exactly as God commands, to the letter, not
looking left or right trying to please or be concerned with other gods.

Because if you refuse to obey, you will be cursed:
- In the city and field, everywhere you go
- To will produce fruit in your body, ground, and flocks.
- In Thy basket and they store
- When you come in and go out

The Lord will hurt you and consume you with fever, burning, inflammation, the sword, blasting and mildew until you are consumed. Your heaven will become brass and your foundation, iron. Your rain will become powder and dust until you are destroyed. And you will be smitten before your enemies, fighting one way but fleeing seven ways. Your dead body will be meat to the fowls of the air with no one to defend it. The Lord will give you blotchy skin, the itch, where you can't be healed. Madness, blindness, and astonishment of heart. You will grope but no man will save you. Another man will lay with your wife, live in your home and reap from your vineyard. Your flocks will be killed, stolen and given to your enemies. Your children given up for adoption as you witness their joy with others. Your land ravaged by strangers and your oppression constant. Your body destroyed at joint and a rash that covers you head to toe. The Lord will bring you and the king you serve to another nation where you will serve carved idols and become a astonishment, a story to tell. You will spend much and reap little. You will plant a vineyards only the worms will drink. Your olive trees will not produce the oil you desire to anoint yourself. Your children will be taken and your fruit consumed. The stranger you help will become bigger and stronger than you. He shall lend to you and you shall borrow. He will be the head and you shall be the tail. And you will be a sign, wonder and story for your children and their children how you disobeyed God and chose not to worship him, enjoy him and receive abundance. Instead you will desperately serve your enemies for the yoke God has placed upon your neck. The Lord will bring a foreign nation against your land, one without mercy whose words you will not understand to take your land and destroy everything God gave you. The onslaught will be so fierce that the delicate man and woman who once highly esteemed their family will turn on them and eat their flesh to survive.

This is a warning. If you refuse to obey the laws written I this book of law, by the Lord, THY GOD, you will be plagued, diseased, sick and low in number. If you do not obey, the-Lord that rejoiced to lift you up will rejoice in tearing you down. You will live in constant fear of what may be and you will become slaves.

BLESSING OR CURSE

In my 20's, I trained to become a multi-media designer and was blessed to attend one of the best technology centers in the nation. I had so many doors opened to me, it was unbelievable. I was married with children and happy. I worked for a television station for two years, then was offered a higher paying position on salary with benefits. Then it all changed, suddenly. After years of infidelity and sneakiness, I caught my husband cheating on me. I moved out and took our children. I went to an out of state conference and met a man I eventually fell in love with. I didn't sleep with him then but we exchanged numbers. I got a divorce. The man visited me, we broke up. I got raped. I decided to move to Atlanta where God gave me an excellent job and a great place to live. But bad habits came with me and caused me to make worse choices. I went from casually smoking marijuana to habitually using coke. I totaled 6 cars in one year and destroyed my self esteem.

Then I found Jesus by picking up the Bible after a night of desperation and pain. I never looked back. God has blessed me abundantly. If I get off track he gently or not so gently reminds me of where I am supposed to be. I am blessed and highly favored but it could easily be another way.

> *"Know ye that the Lord he is God: it is he that hath made us, and not we ourselves; we are his people, and the sheep of his pasture." Psalms 100:3*

In Context

Make a joyful noise to God and serve him with gladness, come before his presence with singing! God made us, not we ourselves. We are his sheep. Be thankful and bless his name! For the Lord is good, his mercy is everlasting and his truth endures to all generations.

Final Notes

The Lord is blessing everything you do in such a way that doors are going to open for you that don't make sense. But loving you means loving God and trusting him. God promises in Deuteronomy that he will rejoice to bless you and rejoice in cursing you. Scripture says that if you are not for than you are against. This is law. While God's mercy is everlasting, so is his truth. Trust God and obey that you might obtain the blessing and not the curse.

Prayer

Most Gracious and Heavenly Father, we thank you for the opportunity to serve you. We stand in prayer, asking for your guidance. We pray for your direction, protection and overwhelming presence of love, grace, discernment and wisdom. Help us to operate in humility and strength as we walk the way you have directed us to go. Lord help us to choose life. To choose blessing over the curse. To be at peace and content with your will above our own. Lord help us to love you therefore loving ourselves. Help us to forgive ourselves for mistakes of the past and move forward in your strength and blessings.

In Jesus Name, Amen.

Honor

*"Honour thy father and thy mother: that thy days may be long upon the land
which the Lord thy God giveth thee."*
Exodus 20:12

In Context

God spoke: I am your Lord that brought you out of Egypt. You
will have no other Gods before me, no graven image or likeness of
anything in heaven above, the earth beneath or the water beneath the
earth. You will not bow to them, serve them, because I am jealous
and require vengeance up to the third and fourth generations of
those that hate me. I show mercy to those that love and obey me.
Never take the Lord's name in vain for you will be found guilty. Keep
the blessed seventh day (Sabbath day) holy, refusing to allow yourself,
family, servants or stranger in your home to work. The Lord rested
after creating the earth on the Sabbath day. Honor your mother and
father that your days will be long on the earth. Do not kill, commit
adultery, steal, lie or desire what is not yours. Then all the people
heard the thunder, saw the smoke and moved back. They asked
Moses to speak with them because they feared God. God asked
Moses to tell them that they have seen God speak to Moses from
heaven. That they shall have no false gods or carved idols. Instead
you will make an alter of earth that you may sacrifice burnt offerings,
peace offerings, sheep and oxen in all places where I record my name
and I will come and bless you. Neither will you come upstairs to an
alter where you may expose yourself.

HONOR

Honor is a big deal in my family. My mother's parents worked tirelessly and without complaint raising eleven children to be honorable, upstanding citizens. To dishonor a member of the family, an elder at the church or elder period was not tolerated. When you answered the phone, you were to say, "Bradley residence, Stephanie speaking." We were to call our grandparents grandmother and grandfather instead of grandma and grandpa. We were also to answer, "Yes ma'am or No sir."

My grandfather was blind. One time, I turned the channel when he went to the bathroom. When he came out and asked, I lied and said, "No sir, I didn't turn the channel," but I had. My mother heard me and took me upstairs for a butt whoopin' I won't ever forget. We were taught to honor our grandparents and lying didn't honor anyone.

Recently, my grandmother was honored with the key to the city for being one of the only black businesses of her type succeeding. Her honor was a direct result of honoring her place of business and its clients.

"Bless the Lord, O my soul. O Lord my God, thou art very great; thou art clothed with honour and majesty." Psalms 104:1

In Context

Lord you are very great and worthy of honor and majesty! To whom light is like a cloak, and heavens like a curtain, with beams of your chambers in the water, and clouds for chariots. Who walks on the wings of the wind, with angels and ministers of flaming fire. Who laid the unmovable foundations of the earth and covered the deep with water that can rise above mountains. At your rebuke, they fled and at the thunder the ran. They go up by mountain and down by valley to the place created for them. You have set bounds they may not cross and the springs he has made feeds the beasts of the field and the birds of the air. He waters the hill from his chambers, the earth is satisfied with your works. From the grass for cattle to the herb for service men to wine, oil and bread for men. Trees for birds and high hills for wild goats, rocks for conies. He appointed the sun and moon to develop seasons. At night the young lions seek prey, and seek their meat from God. The sun rises, men work, how vast are your works. In wisdom you created it all. The earth reflects your riches. In the sea there are creepy things. They all wait for meat in due season. They work and you provide. When you hide, they are troubled, when you take their air, they die. You replenish the earth with new life. The glory of the Lord shall be forever, the Lord will rejoice in his works. He causes earthquakes by looking at them and volcanoes to erupt at touch. I will sing praises to God as long as I live, he is worthy. When I think of him, my thoughts will be sweet. Let the sinners be consumed and the wicked no more. Bless the Lord, praise the Lord oh my soul.

Final Notes

Honor is usually attributed to kings or persons of high stature. In this lesson God teaches that to honor him is to obey him. We have every reason to obey him if we are aware and ever remembering his works that testify of his greatness each day. From time, to provision, to angels and ministers to nature. Everything we see, know, touch and smell are God. He deserves honor and praise!

Prayer

Lord, we spend our lives seeking the greatest things this world has to offer without realizing the best is at our fingertips, well within reach and willing to rest in our hearts if we allow. Forgive us. Help us to see you as you are, magnificent, all-knowing, loving and worthy of all honor, majesty and praise! Forgive us Lord, we confuse our will with your way and stumble down our own dark paths looking for you in our darkness. Help us to get right on track, in your will and abiding in your way.

In Jesus Name, Amen.

DAY
18

Heart Words

"Pleasant words are as an honeycomb, sweet to the soul, and health to the bones."
Proverbs 16:24

In Context

The preparations of a heart and the spoken response are from God. Men think everything they do is right but God weighs the spirit. Commit your work to God and your thought will be established. The Lord has made it all, even evil men for the day of the wicked. Pride is an abomination to God. It will not go unnoticed. Mercy and truth purge iniquity. When men fear God they run from evil. When a man's ways please God, he will make his enemies be at peace with him. It's better to have less and be holy, then cheat and be rich. A man's heart dictates the way but the Lord navigates the journey. The king is wise and his judgments are fair. A just balance is from God and he will weigh it out. It is an abomination for a king to do evil because his throne was created from righteousness. The king loves a person that speaks truth. The wrath of a king is a messenger of death but a wise man will endure. The kings favor will bring rain and in his presence is life. Wisdom and understanding are more precious than silver and gold. Departing from evil is the choice of wise men who keep their souls from harm. Pride goes before destruction and destruction before a mighty fall. Better to be humble with the low than prideful splitting profits. He that handles a matter wisely and trusts God will be blessed and happy. The wise will be called prudent and the sweetness of his lips increase learning. The intelligent love to learn but fools resent it. The heart of the wise teaches his mouth and adds learning to the lips. Pleasant words are sweet to the soul and health to the bones. A man that goes his own way often leads to destruction. He that labors does so for self and his mouth craves it. An ungodly man digs up evil and in his mouth there is a burning fire. A busybody creates strife and separates good friends. A violent man stirs up trouble and drags his neighbor with him. He closes his eyes to good and concentrates on destruction. A crown of gray-haired glory will rest on the righteous. A man that is slow to anger is better than the strong, and he that rules his spirit can take the city. The lot may rest in a lap but total destruction is of God.

KNOWLEDGE IS POWER

We have the tremendous power to bless others with our words and wisdom but we can easily give away the factory for free if we aren't careful. Anger, resentment, pain and heartache will drive a wedge in any situation but you have the power to turn that thing around with time. Patience in tribulation will help you to maintain a good course and long term relationship allowing you to keep your gifts and the factory.

I remember being so upset with a co-worker for questioning my procedures. It took me years to develop and utilize my strategy not to mention the courage to stand out. He said, "I just don't think that is strategic." I was upset at first, but then realized he just didn't understand. Even though he was trying to mock me, I carefully articulated the why, how and what of the science. He then said, "Well I don't know everything about this." Tensions were still high but rather than fan the fire, I waited a while, asked about another project and kept it pushing.

> *"But he giveth more grace. Wherefore he saith, God resisteth the proud, but giveth grace unto the humble." James 4:6*

In Context

Where does war get birthed? Isn't it from your personal desires? You want what you don't have and even kill for what you want but still don't get it! You launch wars but don't ask for what you want. And when you do ask, you are asking for the wrong reasons, to consume it with lust. Cheaters, didn't you know that befriending the world makes an enemy of God? The scripture is not in vain when it says, the spirit that dwells within lusts to envy. But God gives abundant grace to the humble and resists the proud. So give in to God and the devil will run away. Get closer with God, clean your hands and submit your heart. Be afflicted and mourn. Humble yourself and he will lift you up. Don't speak evil to or about your fellow man because at the same time you are speaking to and of God's law in that way, making yourself a judge. There is only one judge and he has the power to give and take life. Who are you to judge. You make plans for tomorrow but you don't know what tomorrow will bring. For what is your life but a vapor? Here today and gone tomorrow. Instead you should say, God-willing we will see tomorrow. For now, you rejoice in your boasting, but that is evil. Now that you know right, if you do wrong, it is a sin.

Final Notes

Trials, arguments, and accusations will come. It's not what you are up against but how you respond. Humility is always the right way. A patient man that controls his anger is more powerful than the strong and will take the city. That sounds like a recipe for success! Enjoy basking in the presence of God when trials come your way. The devil will run as fast as he can!

Prayer

Most Gracious and Heavenly Father, thank you for the blessing of your presence. Thank you for wisdom, guidance and temperance. Help us to protect our lives, our brands and our strategies with your wisdom. Decrease us and increase you. Help us to be all that you have created us to be. Suture our lips and direct our paths, forgive us when we fail.
In Jesus Name, Amen.

Grumpy

"And call upon me in the day of trouble: I will deliver thee, and thou shalt glorify me." Psalms 50:15

In Context

The mighty Lord has spoken, calling forth the earth, from the rising of the sun to the setting of the same. Out of Zion, the perfection of beauty, God has shined. He will come with great fire, fierce and surrounding him. He is going to call the heavens and the earth to judge his people. Gather my saints to me who have committed to me by sacrifice. For the heavens shall declare his righteousness, for God is the only judge. Hear Israel, as I speak and testify against you, for I am God - your God. I am not concerned about your sacrifices for the cattle on a thousand hills belong to me. Every fowl of the air and beast of the field are mine. If I were hungry, I wouldn't tell you because I own all things. Give the Lord what you owe, thanksgiving and praise, because in the day of trouble I will save you and you will glorify me. But to the wicked, how dare you put my words in your mouth and declare anything? Considering you hate instruction and put my words behind you. You have befriended thieves and allowed your mouth to speak evil against your brother. Remember that I know you and have kept silent, but that I will tear you apart with no one to deliver you. Praise me and keep your mouth in order and you will see the salvation of God.

ALL THE WRONG WORDS

God has been speaking to me about my mouth. He has just pulled me out of the fiery furnace and saved me in the lions den and here I am talking about other people like they have issues. I am thankful

89

for God's patience with me because as a parent I am not sure so I wouldn't have whooped my butt. But, God has given me a warning. I don't have a great story because this is for me today. I am sure I could share some story, but trust me... God is speaking to me right now and I better listen.

"Pray without ceasing."
I Thessalonians 5:17

In Context

You don't need me to tell you about time. You know the day the Lord will come will be like a thief in the night. They say, 'have peace you are safe', but it's not so. You can't escape. But you aren't blind to the truth, this won't be a surprise. You are a child of God. Watch and be sober, don't get caught slipping into darkness. We are to wear faith and love with hope of salvation. Those that sleep and drink do so at night, we are to be awake. Our job is not wrath but to obtain salvation through Jesus. Whether we are awake or sleep, we are called to live together with him. Comfort and edify yourselves amongst each other. Know them that labor among you and over you and hold them in high regard with respect to God. Honor them with love for their works sake and be at peace. Warn the unruly and weak at heart, don't execute an eye for an eye and follow the good and be good to all men. Rejoice. Pray always. Give thanks - this is God's will toward you. Quench not the spirit, appreciate prophesy, judge all things fairly and stay away from all evil. Then the peace of God will fill you leading you into salvation. God is faithful and he will do it. Pray for us. Greet each other with a kiss. Let this be read to all brethren.

Final Notes

We are to be holy. No amount of good deeds will change God's opinion of our behavior. We are his ambassadors of the earth. What we do behind closed doors is just as important as what we do outside. We have an audience of one that has the power to judge. God is faithful and he knows us, all of us. We can rest assured that he is working it out for our good. We must stand in faith, believe him and do good.

Prayer

Most Gracious and Heavenly Father, we submit to you. Please forgive us for our wrongs. Help us to heal our wounds and suture our lips. Help us to shine a bright light on who you are in us. Thank you for blessing us and keeping us. Thank you for protecting us. Thank you for bringing us a mighty long way.
In Jesus Name, Amen.

Bad Days

*"Then this Daniel was preferred above the presidents and princes, because an
excellent spirit was in him; and the king thought to set him over the whole realm."*
Daniel 6:3

In Context

Darius was happy to appoint 125 princes to manage his people.
Above them were three leaders, Daniel amongst them. He was the
kings favorite because he had an excellent spirit within him. The
king wanted to appoint him over his entire kingdom. The others
in leadership tried to find a way to accuse him but he was decent,
upstanding and efficient. They decided that the only way they would
get Daniel in trouble would be to punish him for worshiping God.
So they approached the king, touting a consensus of all leadership
concluded   anyone that bows down to another God that is not
the king in the next 30 days, should be thrown into the lion's den.
They then asked the king to make their suggestion a decree effective
immediately. As soon as Daniel knew the writing was signed, he went
into his house and opened the windows toward Jerusalem, kneeled
and prayed to God offering thanks and praise, as was his tradition
before the decree - doing so three times a day. Then the leaders
approached the king and said, "Didn't you issue a decree against
anyone worshiping another god besides the king? Well Daniel has
defied you and worships his God three times a day. The king was
instantly upset with himself and hoped to deliver Daniel but it was
the law. He cast him into the den of lions stating, "The God you
serve continually will deliver you." The stone was rolled over the
mouth of the cave and the order was sealed with the kings insignia
to prevent a change in Daniels punishment. The king went home and

fasted, restless without sleep or music. Immediately the next morning the king ran to the lions den and called to Daniel, "Oh Daniel, was the God you serve, the Living God able to deliver you?" Daniel responded, "Oh king, live forever! The angels have shut the mouths of the lions who recognize the innocent and have not harmed me, nor have I done harm." The king called for him to be removed from the lions den and no harm came to Daniel because he believed and trusted God. Then those that accused Daniel were thrown into the den of lions along with their children and wives, with only scattered bones to remain of their bodies. The king issued another decree, "Peace! I decree that every person in my kingdom worship the God of Daniel - the true and living God. His kingdom will not be destroyed and he will always have dominion. He delivers and rescues, working signs and wonders in heaven and earth. He has saved Daniel from the lions den. Daniel prospered during the reign of Darius and Cyrus.

He Told Me to Do It
Have you ever wondered why people say, "Don't worry! You will get double for your trouble!" Well, it's true. It's God's promise.

When I was working at the TV station as an on-air designer, building graphics and working the newscast, the president called me into his office. He offered me a position as a sales assistant. I didn't have to take the job but they really wanted me to. They were firing a young lady and the sales rep (highest performing rep at the station personally asked for me after I helped her with a project one day). It sounded, felt like, seemed to be a bad career move. A mentor at the station even pulled me aside and told me not to do it. But in my spirit I heard it was ok and a good move. So, I did it. At first, I hated it. But then my hours became M-F, 8-5. (Yes! No breaking weather for me!) Then, I started making sales commission and learned the art of television advertising (which is tricky if you aren't good with numbers). And I was still designing! Within a couple of months, we got a new president and a new sales manager who promoted me to Marketing Coordinator making me not only the station publicist but also in charge of all external branding! I prospered greatly.

"Instead of shame and dishonor, you will enjoy a double share of honor. You will possess a double portion of prosperity in your land, and everlasting joy will be yours." Isaiah 61:7

In Context
To proclaim the Year of the Lord, the vengeance of our God - to comfort and appoint those that mourn in Zion. To replace their pain with joy that they may be called trees of righteousness, planted by the Lord. They shall rebuild and repair desolate places, strangers will feed your flocks and you shall be called priests. You will eat the riches of Gentiles and in their glory you shall boast yourselves. For your shame, I will give you double and everlasting joy. For I the Lord hate robbery, and love judgment. I will direct their work in truth and I will make an everlasting covenant with them. And their children will be well known as being blessed. I will greatly rejoice in the Lord and my soul will be joyful in my God, he has clothed me with salvation, covered me with righteousness and decked me with ornaments and jewels. As the seasons change and plants spring forth, God will cause righteousness and praise to spring forth before all nations.

Final Notes
A bad day can lead to a double portion in blessings. Stay in faith and trust God and his way - making him your source and your guide. They may throw you in the lions den but in the end it will be you that survives and thrives. Today is just a day and nothing is too big for our God! Trust him to see you through.

Prayer

Most Gracious and Heavenly Father, we come to you in prayer and with praise. You are our strength - the everlasting living God who is sure to save. We trust you and honor you. We love you and bless you. Help us to be all that you have called us to be. You are our rock, our shield, and our exceeding great reward. Lord, we ask for supernatural wisdom and discernment to rain down in abundance that we might serve in your purpose with clarity, efficiency and truth. We ask for a special anointing of your Holy Spirit that we may be perfect conduits of your message and your love. We give you all the praise, all the glory and bless your name.

In Jesus Name, Amen.

Words of Affirmation

"This is the day the Lord has made, We will rejoice and be glad in it."
Psalm 118:24

In Context

Psalm 118 extols the sheer goodness of God and his mercy. Give thanks to the Lord for he is good and his mercy endures forever. Let Israel, the house of Aaron and those that fear the Lord say, "His mercy endures forever!"

Then the writer testifies, "When I was in distress, I cried out to the Lord, he brought me into a spacious place and I won't be afraid. What can people do to me?" He goes on to share that the Lord is with him and will give him victory in the sight of his enemies. It is better to trust in the Lord than men or princes. All the nations surrounded me (even as bees) on every side but in the name of the Lord, I cut them down. I was pushed back and about to fall but the Lord helped me. He is my strength, my defense and my salvation. Shouts of joy and victory resound in the tents of the righteous. The Lord's right hand is lifted high and has done mighty things. I will not die! I will live and proclaim the things the Lord has done. The Lord has chastened me severely but has not given me over to death. Open for me the gates of the righteous, I will enter and give thanks to the Lord. This is the gate the righteous will enter, I will give you thanks for you answered me and become my salvation. The stone the builders rejected has become the cornerstone and it is marvelous in our eyes. The Lord has done it today, let us rejoice and be glad! Lord save us, Lord grant us success. Blessed is he who comes in the name of the Lord, from the house of the Lord we bless you. The Lord is

God and he has made his light shine on us! We festively celebrate and parade to the alter, the Lord is good and his mercy endures forever.

A FOREVER KIND OF PRAISE

Have you ever muttered, "Thank you Jesus" for a small victory? Have you ever wept bitterly thanking God for his mercy? I have done both. But never have I appreciated God more than the day he saved me, when he saw the best in me. Just like the song says, when everyone else around me could only see the worst in me. I've made some huge mistakes in my past. Any group of these issues will make someone want to bite the bullet, but in the midst of my worst self, God's love saved me. I opened the Bible in desperation and heard his voice so clearly tell me it was ok and that he loved me. He sent spiritual teachers, preachers, mentors and saints to fellowship with me, teach me and admonish me. He truly deserves all of the praise. If you find yourself in a trial and it looks like defeat, call on Jesus and watch him work it out! He did it for me and I least deserved it, do I know he will do it for you! My brother has a song called, "It's ok." The chorus repeats, it's ok, it's alright." That song and these moments of God's grace give me a forever kind of praise!

"Let every thing that hath breath praise the Lord. Praise ye the Lord."
Psalms 150:6

In Context

Praise the Lord! Praise him in his sanctuary, in the firmament of his power, for his mighty acts, according to his excellent greatness! Praise him with the psaltry and harp, with the Timberlake and dance, with the stringed instruments and organs, with the high cymbals! Let everything that has breath praise the Lord! Praise ye the Lord.

Final Notes

God is so amazing! He sees us as we will be and not as we are. He has a predestined purpose written all over our lives and every move he makes is strategic. Stop and give him some praise right now because no matter how you feel, he deserves it! Give him glory! Give him praise! His mercy endures forever. Forgive yourself and allow God to forgive you. It's ok, it's alright.

Prayer

Dear Lord, you are awesome and amazing in wonder and power. No amount of research will ever give us a proper insight into who you are and what you do or why you do what you do. All we can do is say "Thank you!" So many times we have failed but you have always been right there to pick us up, dust us off, and help us to keep it pushing. Lord, grant us supernatural wisdom and discernment to glorify you with our hands, feet, heart and mouths on today. Anoint us for your use and help us to be strictly obedient to your will against all inferences of self gratification or what we think is best. Help us to be your hands and feet. Purify our hearts that we may be a perfect conduit of your message and love. We give you all the praise, all the glory and all of the honor.

In Jesus Name, Amen.

Instead of the Pain

"*Friends, when life gets really difficult, don't jump to the conclusion that God isn't on the job. Instead, be glad that you are in the very thick of what Christ experienced. This is a spiritual refining process, with glory just around the corner.*" 1 Peter 4:12-13

In Context

Jesus has been through it all and he understands. Consider these sufferings as a way for God to pull you away from sinful desires and selfishness. God is trying to push you into purpose. Forget the life of partying and pursuit that you chased without reward. Your friends won't understand but that is not for you to be concerned with. Listen to what Jesus has shared with many before you, who, although dead now, will have everlasting life. Stay sober and pray, this world won't be here forever. Love! Be generous to those that are less fortunate.

IN THE MIDST OF PAIN

Purpose will push you to do things no one else can understand. I remember starting a prayer ministry in Virginia. Previously, I'd volunteered at a Christian Television station in Atlanta, manning the prayer lines. It was an amazing experience. For quite a while, I'd felt a strong urge to move to D.C. I even traveled to Baltimore one weekend with my daughters to spy out the land. When the revelation of beginning a prayer ministry hit me, I went all in. I remember my family questioned my judgment as I quit my job, left a house I was purchasing, and pulled my 401k to move into an extended stay hotel in Virginia. I'd gotten a new phone line, printed business cards and waited. No calls. I searched for work in DC, but beyond temp work - none could be found. Three months later, I was penniless and just about homeless. My daughters and I moved to Oklahoma City while family and friends laughed at me. I didn't understand. I knew this was God's will for my life. Why did everything turn out the way it did? I pushed ministry to the side and began working at a local television station. This opportunity transitioned me from design into strategic marketing and public relations over four years. In the last year, I began ministry again with programs for women, young ladies and young men. Shortly after, I began operating my company full time as Moore Marketing and Communications. The pain is always meant to push us into purpose. It is building our muscle of strength allowing us to become more than we ever imagined we would be.

"Now to him who is able to do immeasurably more than all we ask or imagine, according to his power that is at work within us, to him be glory in the church and in Christ Jesus throughout all generations, for ever and ever! Amen."
Ephesians 3:20-21

In Context

Paul considers himself a prisoner of Christ Jesus and a messenger to help the Gentiles understand the magnificence of God and his brilliant plan of salvation. This knowledge is the result of revelation provided by the Holy Spirit. That by revelation we understand God's will for Israel and the Gentiles to join as one body. Although Paul considers himself the least worthy to be a messenger, he acknowledges that this is his responsibility. A message that all were to understand allowed them to approach God with freedom and confidence. He then asks that they do not allow his circumstance to deter their belief in God, then he prays for their strength to believe in God through faith. His prayer also asks that each believer may have power coupled with other believers to recognize there is no accurate way to measure the depth of God's love and he prays that God's love may fill them completely. He finishes his prayer by saying, "Unto him that is able to do immeasurably more than we can ask, think or imagine - according to his power that is at work within us be glory in the church and in Christ Jesus, forever and ever, Amen."

Final Notes

Instead of focusing on the pain or loss we have experienced, we should be excited to share the glory and revelation we have gained by living a life with Jesus. No, it's not easy to see the good when you are celebrating Christmas in a one bedroom hotel room with less than $50 to your name, but it is possible. When we meditate on God and simply choose to trust him and not our situations, we have the will power to get up, give him praise and run toward our purpose like a child chasing bouncy bubbles on a summer day. Yes, some may laugh, snicker, point fingers or mock, but in the end - you win. Keep believing, keep trusting and keep walking with God.

Prayer

Lord Jesus, open our eyes to see the many that surround our many enemies. Help us to trust that the battle is not ours, it is yours. Help us to become strong and mature, reflecting your love and your grace despite our circumstance. Thank you Lord for your provision, protection and direction. For the power of the Holy Spirit that works in us. Help us to give. Help us to chase our purpose. Fill us with your revelation and instruction by Holy Spirit and grant us the courage to obey when no one else understands. Fill us with your power to change lives and be your hands and feet. Fill us with your glory that our lights shine so brightly and our work causes men to glorify you in heaven. Decrease us as you increase and help us to be all that you created us to be. We give you glory, honor and praise.
In Jesus Name, Amen.

DAY
23

Prepared

"That the man of God may be perfect, thoroughly furnished unto all good works." 2 Timothy 3:17

In Context

Note: In the last days, it will be brutal. People will be lovers of themselves and money, rude, unloving, ungrateful and lovers of pleasure rather than lovers of God... having some form of Godliness but denying his power. Stay far away from these people. These are the type that take advantage of unsuspecting women, loaded by sin and weighed down by desire... learning the truth but never applying it. But you know my teaching, way of life, purpose and sufferings- you also know that the Lord rescued me from it all. You must believe and have faith as you have been taught from childhood and believe because of your Holy teachers... believe the scriptures which teach faith in Jesus Christ unto salvation. All scripture is God-inspired, used for teaching, rebuking, correction and training so that the servant of God may be thoroughly equipped for every good work.

A GOOD DEED

God is amazing. He knows the heartbeat, the hair count, the secret petitions within our hearts! He is so amazing! No matter the dream he places within me, I know I can trust God. He is awesome. When you walk with God there is just a knowing in your spirit. You have a faith that others can't always see or understand. You know God is working it out for you when it looks dark and gray. Suffering will come, but the bounce back is beautiful. I had a friend, a beautiful spirit that dedicated her life to Christ. She worked feverishly to accomplish the goals he placed within her heart. Unfortunately, she passed away and many that new her felt lost without her. She was such a shining bright light that you could not help but experience the presence of God when in her atmosphere. Today, I know that God gave her a gift and an assignment of greater joy. One that she could only accomplish in heaven. While on earth, she suffered at the thought of not being or providing adequately for her cause, in heaven I know she not only has all she needs but so much more!

"To be absent from the body is to be present with the Lord."
2 Corinthians 5:8

In Context

If our earthly body is destroyed, we have a home in heaven not built by human hands that cannot be destroyed. While we are in this body, we long for our heavenly body. This is by God's design and we are filled with his Holy Spirit confirming it shall come to pass. In this way we know that as long as we are comfortable in this body we are away from the Lord. We walk by faith, not by sight. Our preference is to be with God, so we make it our goal to please him whether we are in heaven or on earth. Because we are all held accountable for our actions in this body, whether good or bad. For this reason, we make an argument to help lead others to Christ. We desire you take pride in what is in the heart as opposed to what is seen. To others we may seem crazy for believing that Christ died for us but we know what is true. If anyone is in Christ they are a new creature and the old man is done away. This is a gift from God, salvation through Christ that our sins may not be counted against us. Therefore we are Christ's ambassadors and his appeal to save a dying world comes through us. Be reconciled to God, that the sinless nature we inherit from Christ for the sinful nature he adopted from us will lead us into all righteousness.

Final Notes

Prepared for our purpose! God is doing a new thing, from the knowledge of scripture to the trial of faith, to the power of the Holy Spirit - God's everlasting gift of forgiveness and salvation are badges of honor we should be proud to wear. If our father were an honored man and highly esteemed among his peers for heroic acts, no doubt we would be proud with peacock feathers, bullhorn and a story to tell. Doors of entitlement, opportunity and generosity would be available to us. In the same way, we should be so delighted to share our good fortune to be adopted and dripped in righteousness we don't deserve that leads not just us but all who accept him in their hearts to salvation. The blessings we receive in connection to the power of His Name and His Word are endless and innumerable. What an honor it is to be prepared to serve God, the creator of the universe in such a mighty way!

Prayer

Dear Most Gracious and Heavenly Father, we honor you and thank you for your invaluable gift. Help us to be the ambassadors of your story, your glory and your praise! Reconcile us to you, forgive us and consecrate us that we might be a perfect conduit of your message and your love. Help us to choose you over the temptations that desire, greed and fame present. Protect our hearts and minds and clear our circle of influence. Let those that remain be your servants bringing glory to your name. Encamp your angels of protection around us.

In Jesus Name, Amen.

Into the Promised Land

Thankful to God

"He threw himself at Jesus' feet and thanked him—and he was a Samaritan."
Luke 17:16

In Context

Jesus said, "Things that cause people to stumble are bound to come but woe to the one it comes through. It would be better for them to be thrown into the sea with a millstone tied around their neck then to cause one of these little ones to stumble. So watch yourselves. If your brother or sister sins against you rebuke them, if they repent forgive them. Even if they sin against you seven times in a day and they still come back and say I repent, forgive them." The apostles responded, "Increase our faith!"

Jesus answered, "If you have a mustard seed of faith and say to this mulberry tree be uprooted, and go into the sea, it will obey. Suppose one of you has a servant plowing or looking after the sheep. Will he say to the servant when he comes in from the field, 'Come along now and sit down to eat'? Won't he rather say, 'Prepare my supper, get yourself ready and wait on me while I eat and drink; after that you may eat and drink'? Will he thank the servant because he did what he was told to do? So you also, when you have done everything you were told to do, should say, 'We are unworthy servants; we have only done our duty.'" Jesus was on his way to Jerusalem when ten men with leprosy approached him from afar and asked for him to heal them. "Jesus, Master, have pity on us!" When Jesus saw them he said to them, "Go show yourselves to the priests," and as they went they were healed. One of the men, realizing he was healed, turned back to thank Jesus. He fell on his knees and thanked Jesus at his feet, and he was a Samaritan. "Were there not ten? Where are the other nine? No one has returned to give praise to God except this foreigner. Rise and go, your faith has made you whole." Another time, the Pharisees asked Jesus when the kingdom of God would come. Jesus answered that it is not something you can see and call out because it is here and now in your midst. Then he turned to his disciples and added that there will be a time when men seek the Lord but he will not be found. They will try to say he is here or there but it won't be true. In the same way the flood of Noah happened suddenly while people were unexpectedly doing their normal daily activities, or as when Sodom and Gomorrah were destroyed by fire suddenly, so shall the Lord be revealed suddenly - unexpected. On that day, leave it all behind and don't look back. If you try to preserve your life you will lose it but if you lose it you will gain life. In that day two will be in bed but one will be taken and the other left. In the same way, two women will be working together and one will be left. After hearing this, the disciples asked, "Where Lord?" He responded, "Where there is a dead body, there the vultures will gather."

WHERE THE VULTURES GATHER

Have you ever known you were in the wrong place at the wrong time doing the wrong thing? How blessed we are that the moment we were at our worst wasn't the moment God chose to come gather his people!

I remember a time, living in Atlanta, when I knew, I was all the way wrong and couldn't find right. I would pray before I left my house to buy coke that I would make it home without being arrested, I would pray on my way to the drug dealers house that I wouldn't get raped, I would pray on the way home that the high wouldn't be too much for my body. The entire time I knew I was wrong I begged God not to kill or harm and to even protect me. Eventually I began to read the Bible and pray more earnestly for my recovery. It was a slow process with lots of failures but eventually as my faith increased, God brought me out. Every time I failed, he would remind me that his grace was enough.

"For my grace is sufficient, for in your weakness is my strength made perfect." I Corinthians 12:9

In Context

I Corinthians 12 is a letter written by Paul to Timothy. He opens by stating he prefers not to address the issue at hand in such a way but feels compelled to. He notes that while he has performed wonderful acts, he is also a fool. This handicap he has been given was given that he might remain humble and trust in the strength of God when he is weak. So rather than beat himself up, he gives God glory for God's perfect strength. He goes on to write that while he is defending himself, he wishes the shoe was on the other foot. He wishes that the person he has elected to serve appreciated his service and would defend him when his work was doubted. Because he whom he served knows better than anyone else what a majestic work he has done and it is not second rate in the least. He asks if he or anyone he connected him to has harmed him or done him a disservice.

He apologizes for being a burden to him in his weakness. Finally, he concludes, I am not here to receive what you have, I am here to serve YOU with my gift. I would give anything to serve you with gladness... but the more I love you, the more you hate me. Why are you whispering behind my back that I betrayed you? Nothing could be more ridiculous. I am not here to gain your approval for my approval comes from God alone. I can't and won't stand in your way on your journey to personal growth. I hated the thought of coming to speak to you about this, because I feared the fighting would end it all in an ugly way. But in the end, I don't desire another opportunity to be the butt of your jokes among friends who choose deceit as a way of life.

Final Notes

Be not deceived, God is not mocked. Yes, God is good, gracious, wonderful and majestic. But he deserves your praise and honor. So many times we forget to come back and say Thank you Lord for the victory on today. They could have fired me but they didn't. They could have killed me but they didn't. Instead, like the nine we skip away to do our own thing without so much as a thank you. We are to serve God without expecting gifts, we are to fear God who made heaven and earth. We are to Thank God. His mercy is brand new every morning and it endures forever and ever. He comes like a thief in the night, so we are to watch ourselves and forgive others as he has forgiven us.

Prayer

Most Gracious and Heavenly Father, thank you. We can never say it enough. So from a pure place in our hearts we extend the highest praise, Hallelujah! You have been better than we deserve and it is an honor to receive the gift of salvation. Forgive us of our sins, decrease us and increase you. Help us to be more like you each day. And Lord, help us to be watchful, sober and ready when you arrive.
In Jesus Name, Amen.

Poor Friends

"That person is like a tree planted by streams of water, which yields its fruit in season and whose leaf does not wither— whatever they do prospers."
Psalm 1:3

In Context
Blessed is the one who does not join forces with the wicked, or stand and watch with sinners, or hang with those that make fun of people. But his delight is in the law of the Lord and in his law does he meditate day and night. That person is like a tree planted by streams of water that yields fruit in its season and who's leaf does not whither - whatever they do prospers. Not so the wicked, they are like chaff that the wind blows away. Therefore the wicked will not stand in judgment, nor sinners in the assembly of the righteous. For the Lord watches over the way of the righteous, but the way of the wicked leads to destruction.

<u>CHOOSE LIFE</u>
Even today, amidst all of my blessings, I have to remind myself of this. That every choice, changes my direction. I am either going higher or lower. If you were to chart your decision making process on a graph that represented 10 minute intervals (to get up early, to clean the kitchen, to call a perspective client, etc.) and looked at the chart of up and down throughout the day. You would be able to categorize the way your day went. If you were to do it each day, you could analyze your week and month creating a quantitative score and projection on where you are going. So, if you were to do this based solely on spiritual conviction, are you choosing life? I have to ask myself this. I have purposely created a life that is immersed in

purpose, or what I feel is God's purpose for me. But I wonder, am I always choosing life in the little decisions. The hard truth is maybe not...

One such example is an event I helped plan in minimal ways. One of the speakers I invited did not bring her A game. I was somewhat embarrassed but realized it wasn't a sole reflection on me. In fact, my mother taught this woman in school and I spoke to her via text about it. Her response was comical yet inappropriate. I thought it was so funny I forwarded it to a mutual friend but felt guilty immediately. Here I am trying to encourage others to be more like Christ but I am handling my personal life wrong. I vowed to be better and do better.

"To whom much is given, much is required." Luke 12:48

In Context

When a large crowd filled with thousands of people gathered (so large they were trampling one another) Jesus began by speaking to his disciples:

"Be careful not to be contaminated by the attitudes of those close to you, Pharisee false sincerity. You will be discovered no matter how cleverly you attempt to disguise it. You can't behind a religious mask forever; eventually you will slip and be known. You can't whisper one thing in private and confess another in public. The day is coming when the truth will spread like wildfire all over town. I say this to you as a friend. Don't get pushed by spiritual bullies to be silent or become fake. Fear God who holds your body and soul, do not fear those that can only harm your body. If God cares so dearly for an inexpensive canary, how much more does he value you? He even knows the numbers of hairs on your head. Don't be afraid of a bully. You are worth more than a million canaries.

Honor me before men and I will honor you before God's angels. If you act like you don't know me, I will do the same to you before God's angels. If you disrespect me in ignorance it can be forgiven. But if you purposely disrespect me and grieve the Holy Spirit, it will not be overlooked."

A man cried, "My brother is cheating me. Make him give me my fair share of the inheritance!" Jesus responded, "Sir, what makes it my business to become a mediator or judge in this matter?"

He said to the people, "Beware of greed. Life is not defined by the amount of money you have, a little or a lot." He told the a story. "A farmer was doing well. His crops exceeded the space he had to store them. So he tore down all of his barns to build bigger ones with the intent to retire early. He patted himself on the back noting how well he'd done. Instantly, God appeared to take his life. He remarked, "You fool. Tonight you die! Now who will get your profit?" This is the consequence to those who fill their lives with self rather than God.

He spoke to his disciples: "Don't be so critical about what you eat or wear. It's not important. Do you see the ravens, carefree? God cares more for you then they and they are well cared for. Look at the wildflowers. Beautifully adorned, even ten men in the best tailored suits can't compare to their exquisite natural beauty. If God cares for them, certainly he will care for you. My goal is to get you to calm down and have faith that God is going to care for you. This will stop you from always trying to get and focus on giving! God is going to take care of your every need. People that don't know God question where their next will come from but you know him. So trust him."

"Be good to the poor, give. When you invest in the poor, you are opening a savings and trust in heaven that can't be stolen. Where you invest is where you want to be and where you will be."

"Be ready. Live as though you were a servant waiting on his master to return from honeymoon. Once he arrives to find you waiting, he will get in the kitchen and cook for you, then serve and eat with you. No matter when he arrives - they are awake and blessed! The house owner that is lazy and careless will stay out late, leaving the door unlocked and get robbed when they least expect it. In the same way, if you aren't alert and waiting for Jesus, he will show up unexpectedly."

Peter then asked, "Is this story just for us or everyone?" Jesus responded, "Who is the dependable manager? Doing as he should when the master isn't looking? Is he the one taking his authority too far being mean to the servants, throwing parties and acting a fool? When the master arrives he will send him back to servitude. Better is a servant trying to serve in ignorance than one who serves corruptly. R The ignorant will get a slap on the wrist, the cunning will be thrashed. To whom much is given, much is required."

"I have come to make major changes on this earth - to set it on fire! In fact, I wish it were done right now. I am turning everything right side up. I am not hear to ply nice and make everyone comfortable. In fact, I am here to do the opposite. Every house will be divided."

He turned to the crowd. "You have the knowledge to predict the weather with accuracy. Why are you not able to tell the season of God has changed? You don't have to be a genius, just use common sense. The kind of sense that would make you settle out of court with the one you have offended rather than be taken to jail or forced to pay every last penny of the fine. That is the kind of decision I am asking you to make."

Final Notes

Play time is over. God is trusting us to be his hands and feet on this earth. We are his ambassadors. Rather than Chase a life of false pretense building bigger barns, we are to be investing in a heavenly savings and trust. The type of company we keep can shift who we are. Peer pressure and fake ways will eventually be exposed, so we are to measure our friends and fellowship with people that are evenly yoked. You may not be buying the best clothing or eating at the finest establishments but you will be well cared for and highly favored.

Prayer

Most Gracious and Heavenly Father, help us to choose friends that are approved by you. We can't always see their motives, we come to you praying for supernatural wisdom and discernment to not only recognize but to also make the proper choices. Lord, we thank you for blessing us with the presence of your Holy Spirit. We thank you for mercy and grace. Help us to be givers and not takers, doers and not talkers, believers and not pretenders. Lord, you are our rock, our shield and our exceeding great reward. Bless us to be a blessing. Direct our paths and make them straight. We give you glory, honor and praise.

In Jesus Name, Amen.

Into the Promised Land

DAY
26

Environment

"By day the Lord went ahead of them in a pillar of cloud to guide them on their way and by night in a pillar of fire to give them light, so they could travel by day or night." Exodus 13:21

In Context

God ordered Moses to consecrate every first born to him. Whether man or animal, the first born was to be dedicated to God. Moses instructed the people, "Always remember this day. This is the day God brought you out of Egypt, out of slavery. Don't eat any bread with yeast." You are leaving in the month of Abib, when God brings you into your promised land flowing with milk and honey, always remember this time. For 7 days, no bread with yeast. Then on the 7th day, you are to host a festival to God. Only unraised bread for 7 days. There is not to be a sign of it anywhere. Remind your children, "This is because of what God did for me out of Egypt. This day observance will be like a sign on your hand, A memorial between your eyes, and the teaching of God on your mouth. It was with a powerful hand that God brought you out of Egypt, remember this day year after year." He then told them that when they get into the land of Canaan, their promised land, that they are to give God their first fruit. Their first born son and any animal born to them. A donkey can be traded for a sheep but it's neck must be broken. If your son asks you why, explain that when God powerfully brought us out of Egypt, when Pharaoh refused to let us go, he did so by killing every first born son. It so happened that after Pharaoh refused to let them go that God did not lead them out through the land of the Philistines, because God thought that if the people encountered war, they will go back to Egypt. So he led them in military formation, on

119

the wilderness road, looping around the Red Sea. They carried the bones of Joseph with them, as they promised. Joseph told them God would hold them accountable if they did not bring his bones with them out of Egypt. They moved from Succoth to Etham the edge of the wilderness. By day the Lord went ahead of them in a pillar of cloud to guide them on their way and by night in a pillar of fire to give them light, so they could travel by day or night. The pillar of cloud by day and pillar of fire by night never left them.

SAFE IN HIS HANDS

In a lot of ways, Atlanta was an Egypt for me. I was enslaved by image. I wanted to be what everyone else thought I should be and my soul was paying the cost. When I finally moved to D.C., I thought I was coming into my promised land but it was my wilderness. It was tough, but by the grace of God, I made it. God brought me out with a powerful hand because Satan thought he had me. I didn't have to go to war, I just had to withstand a season of hardship before God transitioned me into a greater place. He was with me every step of the way, never leaving my side.

"When you cross the Jordan and live in the land which the LORD your God is giving you to inherit, and He gives you rest from all your enemies around you so that you live in security," Deuteronomy 13:12

In Context

Observe the following rules closely in the land God has given you to possess. Ruthlessly get rid of every vile place of worship in the land you are entering to possess, no matter where it is, get rid of it. Tear it all down! Stay away and don't let what happened there contaminate the worship of God. Instead find the perfect place that God would enjoy and mark it clearly that all the tribes will worship in this common place. Assemble, worship, make offerings and pay tithes there. Celebrate everything you and your family accomplish under the blessing of God, your God. Don't keep doing it your way. You have not yet crossed over into your promised land, the land of rest, your inheritance, God's blessing. But the minute you cross over, God is going to give you rest from all of your enemies. You will be able to settle down and live in safety. From then on, at the place

God has directed you to worship in his name, bring your offerings and tithes, your children, families, friends and the strangers that live among you. Celebrate there. But be careful. You can't just give to any worship establishment but you must give to the one God has directed you to. You can slaughter and eat non-sacrificial animals. It don't eat their blood. Pour it out on the ground like water. Nor may you eat your tithe in grain, new wine, nor the first born of your herds and flocks, nor your offerings. Your offerings must be eaten in the place God chooses with your family, friends and the stranger. All men are welcome to eat there. Never ever neglect the stranger in your promised land. When God expands your territory as he promised he would do, and you are far away but hungry, go ahead and eat as though you would in the place God ordered you to eat. All men are welcome to eat. Whatever you do, don't eat the blood. There is life in the blood. Pour it out like water. Don't eat it so that you and your descendants will have a good life. Do what is right in God's eyes. Listen and obey so that you will enjoy a good life, you and your children - doing what is right in the eyes of God for a long, long time. When God displaces the people who's land you are invading don't get curious and wonder what it is like to worship their gods... after they have been destroyed before you. They are evil in the sight of God! Do exactly as God commands when he commands it.

Final Notes

God IS going to bring you into your land flowing with milk and honey. He will be with you every step of the way. But, just as he blesses you he expects you to walk in strict obedience, following directions and staying away from evil. This will bless you and generations to come.

Prayer

Lord, we thank you for your utmost generosity towards us. We
are blessed beyond imagination. Help us to remember your
instructions and your will. Help us put you before ourselves and
to never neglect the stranger among us. Help us to be all that you
created us to be, adhering to your command. Forgive us when
we fall short and allow your Holy Spirit to guide us along the
way. Help us to create a straight path for the Lord to travel as we
continue our journey. We love you and bless you.
In Jesus Name, Amen.

DAY
27

Emotion

"Then the Spirit of the LORD came powerfully upon him. He went down to Ashkelon, struck down thirty of their men, stripped them of everything and gave their clothes to those who had explained the riddle. Burning with anger, he returned to his father's home." Judges 14:12

In Context

Samson's parents raised him exactly as God instructed, down to his mother's diet in the womb and his grooming. As a result, he grew to be a man with extraordinary strength. In this chapter, Samson saw a beautiful woman, a Philistine woman, in the city of Timnah. He came home and told his parents, "I saw a beautiful woman and I want to marry her." His parents replied, "Isn't there a young lady among our people that you find attractive? Do you have to choose a young lady from the uncircumcised Philistines?" But Samson replied, "Get her for me. I don't want anyone else, she's the right one." Samson's parents had no idea that this was God's strategic plan at work to avenge the Philistine's who were masters to the Israelites at the time. So Samson and his parents went down to Timnah. Samson came across a vineyard and a young lion approached ready to attack, but Samson grabbed the lion by the jaw and ripped him open by the power of God. His parents did not see and he did not mention the incident to them. He then went down to speak to the Timnah woman, in his eyes, she was the one. Days later, when he came back to get the woman, he went by the vineyard where the lions carcass lay. To his surprise, when he looked inside the carcass had a swarm of bees and honey inside. He scooped up a handful of honey and ate it as he went. He caught up with his parents and shared the honey with them, not revealing the source of its origin. His father went down to make arrangements with the woman while he prepared a feast, this was the custom. The people were wary of Samson, so they sent thirty local men to mingle with him. Samson challenged the men to solve a riddle before the seven day feast ended, promising each of them a pair of fine linen garments and fine linen clothing. They replied, "Tell us your riddle." He said, "From the eater came something to eat. From the strong came something sweet." After 3 days, they still couldn't solve the riddle. They turned to Samson's wife and threatened her. They told her that they would burn her father's house down if she did not worm the answer out of her husband. Did she bring him there just to rob her people?" She blamed Samson. She turned to him in tears saying, "You don't love me. You hate me! You told a riddle to my people and you won't even tell me the answer." He told her, "I haven't even told my parents - why would I tell you?" She cried for the entire feast. On the seventh day, he broke down and told her. She ran to tell her people. Before sunset the men came to Samson and said, "What is sweeter than honey? What is stronger than a lion?" Samson said, "If you hadn't plowed my heifer, you wouldn't know that!" He grew angry and filled with the power of God, he went down to Ashkelon, killed thirty men, stripped them and gave their clothing to those that solved the riddle. Angry and upset, Samson returned home with his parents. Samson's wife became the bride of the best man at the wedding.

CHEATING YOURSELF
Emotions will make you cheat yourself out of some real blessings. Whether the emotion is sadness coupled with depression or anger mixed with violence, we all make mistakes!

When I was about 15, I wanted to go and party with some friends. My mother was angry with me for misbehaving and I was angry at her for being angry with me. I called her a bitch. Before I knew it, my mother had grabbed me by my hair and had me up against the kitchen wall. I remember looking at the dishes in the sink. The pots and pans on the stove, then the rage in her face. I realized at that moment, my feet weren't touching the ground. She was right, I didn't have time to call 911 (lol). She used to always say that if I wanted to fight we could but there would be no way I would make it to the phone fast enough to call 911. Of course, she would never fight me but she would let me know what would and would not be tolerated.

I know that being an angry teen cheated me out of the loving relationship I could have experienced with my mother. I wish we were closer then maybe my adulthood would have started differently. While the thought of what it could have been makes me sick with regret, I am happy because I managed to build a relationship with her and Christ.

"Amnon became so obsessed with his sister Tamar that he made himself ill. She was a virgin, and it seemed impossible for him to do anything to her." 2 Samuel 13:2

In Context

Over time, Amnon fell deeply in love with his brother's sister, Tamar. They were all the children of David. He lusted for her until he made himself sick. He knew she was a virgin and there would never be an opportunity to consume his lust. Amnon's cousin was also his advisor. He asked Amnon, why he, the son of the king looked so pitiful each morning. He explained that he'd fallen in love with Absalom's sister. Immediately his cousin devised a plan. "Pretend you are ill. Tell your father you need your sister to care for you. That you would like her to prepare a meal before you and feed you." Amnon did exactly as instructed. David asked Tamar to cook and serve her brother. She did. But when she tried to feed him, he refused to eat it. He told her to send everyone from the room. They left. Then he instructed her to bring the food into his bedroom to feed him. But when she tried to feed him, he grabbed her and said, "Come to bed with me, my sister." She said, "No, my brother, don't force me! No such thing must be done in Israel. Don't do this. Where would I get rid of my disgrace? And you would be like one of the wicked fools in Israel. Please, speak to the king, he will not keep me from you." But he refused to listen to her and since he was stronger than her, he raped her. Immediately after his love for her turned to an even stronger hatred. "Get up and get out!" She screamed, "No! That would be an even greater wrong than what you've already done to me!" But he again refused to listen to her. He called his personal servant and told him to remove this woman and bolt the door after her. She was wearing an ornate colorful robe as the virgin daughters of the king wore. She put her hands on her face and wept loudly as she left. Her brother Absalom saw her and asked, "Has your brother Amnon been with you? He is your brother, calm down, don't take it to heart." Tamar lived in her brother Absalom's house a desolate woman. When David found out he was furious. Absalom never spoke of it to Amnon good or bad but he hated him for what he did to his sister. Two years later, Absalom's sheepshearers were near the border of Ephraim. He invited all of his brothers to dinner. He invited his father and his servants but the king refused attendance due to being a burden. Absalom insisted but King David refused and gave him a blessing. Absalom then insisted that King David allow Amnon to come. Resisting, he relented and allowed him to go. So Absalom gave an order to his servants, "When Amnon gets drunk, I will tell you to strike him down. Do it, this is my instruction. Be brave, do not fear, be strong." The servants did as instructed. Then all the kings sons mounted their mules and ran away. The report came to King David that Absalom murdered all his sons. But the advisor and cousin of Amnon assured King David that he'd only murdered Amnon. That it has been his plot and plan since the day he raped his sister. Absalom fled. The kings sons came home to confirm the servants story. They were all very sad and wept bitterly. Absalom fled to Geshur and lived for three years. King David longed for him because he'd long ago been consoled for Amnon's death.

Final Notes
God is God over everything. He was there when Samson got tricked... it was even his plan. He was there when Tamar got raped and he was there when Amnon got murdered. God was there when David and all his sons wept bitterly for Amnon and God was there when Absalom fled in fear. He knows everything we go through. It all has purpose. Pain won't change the outcome. David could have had Amnon killed but he didn't. He could have chased after Absalom. But he didn't. The situations we face may challenge us. The more important factor is how we react.

Prayer
Lord Jesus, please help us to be what you have designed us to be.
Help us to make the right choice in tough situations, managing
our emotions even when they threaten to subside in ugly and
unmanageable ways. Be a fence all around us and protect us from
all hurt, harm and danger,.
In Jesus Name, Amen.

DAY
28

My Routine

"When Daniel knew that the document had been signed, he went to his house where he had windows in his upper chamber open toward Jerusalem. He got down on his knees three times a day and prayed and gave thanks before his God, as he had done previously." Daniel 6:10

In Context

Darius was happy to appoint 125 princes to manage his people. Above them were three leaders, Daniel amongst them. He was the kings favorite because he had an excellent spirit within him. The king wanted to appoint him over his entire kingdom. The others in leadership tried to find a way to accuse him but he was decent, upstanding and efficient. They decided that the only way they would get Daniel in trouble would be to punish him for worshiping God. So they approached the king, touting a consensus of all leadership concluded   anyone that bows down to another God that is not the king in the next 30 days, should be thrown into the lion's den. They then asked the king to make their suggestion a decree effective immediately. As soon as Daniel knew the writing was signed, he went into his house and opened the windows toward Jerusalem, kneeled and prayed to God offering thanks and praise, as was his tradition before the decree - doing so three times a day. Then the leaders approached the king and said, "Didn't you issue a decree against anyone worshiping another god besides the king? Well Daniel has defied you and worships his God three times a day. The king was instantly upset with himself and hoped to deliver Daniel but it was the law. He cast him into the den of lions stating, "The God you serve continually will deliver you." The stone was rolled over the mouth of the cave and the order was sealed with the kings insignia to prevent a change in Daniels punishment. The king went home and fasted, restless without sleep or music. Immediately the next morning the king ran to the lions den and called to Daniel, "Oh Daniel, was the God you serve, the Living God able to deliver you?" Daniel responded, "Oh king, live forever! The angels have shut the mouths of the lions who recognize the innocent and have not harmed me, nor have I done harm." The king called for him to be removed from the lions den and no harm came to Daniel because he believed and trusted God. Then those that accused Daniel were thrown into the den of lions along with their children and wives, with only scattered bones to remain of their bodies. The king issued another decree, "Peace! I decree that every person in my kingdom worship the God of Daniel - the true and living God. His kingdom will not be destroyed and he will always have dominion. He delivers and rescues, working signs and wonders in heaven and earth. He has saved Daniel from the lions den. Daniel prospered during the reign of Darius and Cyrus.

DOING WHAT IS RIGHT WHEN NO ONE IS LOOKING

It's easy to do what you think is right when everyone is paying attention, but what about when they aren't?

When I worked for a national magazine, I would go to a secret closet and pray each day on my breaks. I wasn't praying for me, I was praying for the company I served. I knew we could serve our clients with a faster turnaround time. We could do in 24 hours what we were quoting we could do in 2 or 3 days. When I began to openly place scriptures on my desk at work, and pray in that closet, I was attacked by one of the supervisors that hired and promoted me. He was gay and an atheist. He pulled me in his office one day to make sure I understood that. I told him the God I serve loves everyone. Regardless of attack, I continued to pray for higher quality and a stronger work ethic in the office. (Actually, a lot of our artists were wasting a majority of the work day doing nothing or taking too long on their ads). I often finished my workload by noon and would grab ads from struggling artists who got more complicated projects. Well, eventually I was rectified with that boss AND they converted to flipping ads in 24-hours. I knew that was God and that he'd heard my prayer. After that, I knew my assignment there was over and I moved to D.C.

"But when you pray, go away by yourself, shut the door behind you, and pray to your Father in private. Then your Father, who sees everything, will reward you."
Matthew 6:6

In Context

Jesus shares a message interpreted as: Don't show the world your righteousness, as if flaunting it. Otherwise, you will have no reward in heaven. Don't blow horns or trumpets when you give to the needy, don't let your right hand see what your left is doing. Give in secret and your father will reward you openly. Don't pray as hypocrites do, openly before all to be seen by all. Instead pray in secret and your father who hears in secret will reward you. Don't keep on babbling with many words because your father knows what you need before you ask him. This is how you should pray: Our Father, who art in heaven, hallowed be thy name, Give us this day our daily bread, forgive us our debts as we forgive our debtors, lead us not into temptation but deliver us from evil. Forgive those that sin against you, in this way God will also forgive you for your sins. But if you do not, your father will not forgive you. When you do fast, do not look somber as some do. Instead put oil on your face and wash it, God who sees you in secret will reward you openly. Do not store up treasures on earth that can be stolen. Instead, store up the type of treasures that cannot be stolen, for where your treasure is your heart will be also. The eye is the lamp of the body, if there is light your whole body is in light but if darkness, your whole body is in darkness. How dark that darkness is. No one can serve two masters, either you love the one and hate the other or you will be devoted to one and despise the other. You cannot live God and money. Do not worry about your life. What you will eat, or wear. Is not your life more than what you wear or eat? Look at the birds, they don't sow or reap and cannot collect a harvest, yet God feeds them. Are you not much more valuable than they are? Who can add a single hour to their lives worrying? Why do you worry about clothes, look at the flowers, they do not labor or spin. Yet there is not even Solomon in all his splendor was adorned as one of these. If that is how God clothes the flowers, which grow today but are tomorrow thrown into the fire, how much more would he clothe you- oh ye of little faith. So don't worry saying what shall we eat, what shall we drink, what shall we wear? For the pagans worry about these things and God knows you have need of them. But seek ye first his kingdom and his righteousness and all these things shall be added unto you. Therefore do not worry about tomorrow, tomorrow worries about itself, sufficient for the day is it's own trouble.

Final Notes

Whether you have been thrown into the lion's den, the fiery furnace, are low on finance and without food or adequate clothing; a sincere relationship with God will see you through. If you aren't just putting on a show but truly worshiping God in secret, God will bless you.

Prayer

Most Gracious and Heavenly Father, as we enter our secret place to give you praise, please forgive us and help us to forgive others. Lord Jesus, help us to store treasure that cannot be stolen, grant us the right mind and spirit to do your will above our own. Help us to speak life over our futures and the futures of others. Lord, bless those that are sick. Bless those that are hurting. Bless those that are in need. Help us to be your hands and feet in the earth.
We love you.
In Jesus Name, Amen.

DAY 29

Loving Me

*"For God so loved the world, that he gave his only begotten son that whosoever
believes in him shall not perish but have everlasting life." John 3:16*

In Context

Nichodemus, A prominent leader among the Jews approached Jesus
late in the night. He told him, "We know that you are a man sent
from God, otherwise you could not do all that you've done or teach
what you've taught." "You are right," said Jesus. "Take it from me,
only a person that is born again can see that I am pointing to God's
kingdom." But Nichodemus was confused. "How can someone
be born again if they've already been born and are grown up. No
one can re-enter the womb. What do you mean when you say born
again?" Jesus responded, "You are not listening. I'll say it again unless
a person submits to this original creation-a baptism into new life,
it's not possible to enter God's kingdom. When you look at a baby,
it's something that you can see and touch. But the life inside the
baby that is being formed, you cannot see or touch-that's because
it is a living spirit." Jesus went on to share the comparison of the
Holy Spirit to the wind and how one can't determine its origin
or destination. But this confused Nichodemus even more. Jesus
countered, "You're a respected teacher of Israel and you don't know
these basic things. Listen carefully, I'm speaking the whole truth with
you. I speak only what I know by experience. I give witness to only
what I have seen with my own eyes-there's nothing second hand here,
no hearsay. Yet, instead of facing the evidence and accepting it, you
procrastinate with these questions. If I tell you things that are plain
before your face and you don't believe me, what use is there in telling
you things you can't see-the things of God. No one has ever gone

133

up into the presence of God except the one who came down from that presence - the Son of Man. In the same way that Moses lifted the serpent in the desert so people could have something to say and then believe it is necessary for the Son of Man to be lifted up and everyone who sees him, trusting and expectant, will gain a real life-eternal life.

God loved us so much that he gave his son, his only son and he did it so that no one would be destroyed just by believing in him. Anyone can have a whole and lasting life. God didn't go to all the trouble of sending his son just to point an accusing finger, telling the world how bad it was. He actually came to help to put the world in a right space again. Anyone who trusts in him is acquitted and anyone who refuses to trust him has long since been under the death sentence without knowing it. Why? Because that person failed to believe in Jesus Christ when he was introduced to him. This is the mess that we are in: God sent his light into the world but men and women ran for the darkness. They went for the darkness because they weren't really interested in pleasing God. People that do evil are afraid that they'll be exposed if they come too close to the light. But anyone working and living in truth and reality welcomes the light, that the work of God can be seen." After speaking with Nichodemus, Jesus was relaxing on the Judean countryside with his disciples, he was also baptizing. John the Baptist had followers that saw Jesus as their competition. But John corrected them stating, "It's not possible for a person to succeed in the work of God without having help and you were there when I told the Pharisees that I'm not the Messiah, I am simply the one to get things ready. In fact, it's an honor for me to be at his side. I'm genuinely happy. The one who gets the bride is technically the bride groom and the bride groom's friend is the best man. How could I be jealous when I know that the wedding is finished and the marriage is off to a wonderful start? My cup is running over, it is his time to shine. God himself is the truth. God loves Jesus immensely. If you trust him, you receive his blessings - if you don't, you live in angry darkness.

IN LOVE WITH ME

The gift of life is to believe in Jesus and live a life that you love. It won't always be respected by your peers but if you have a relationship with Jesus Christ you won't need to be respected by your peers because you will live and breathe off the love of Christ alone. There was a time when Jesus called me to post a scripture every day and he wanted me to do that with my picture every day and I did. Every scripture at the end of it had - #Believe. Some days I got likes, some days I received none. Either way, I was going to be obedient. God wanted me to put a banner on my back and let others know, I belong to him. When you fully give your life to Christ you stop worrying about what your friends or family say and think and look to God for your guidance. You will trust that he is bringing the right people at the right time to bless you. All you have to do is believe. I am living a life of faith. Leaning and depending on him to do what he promised he would do. You will fall madly in love with who you are when you trust him.

"Your beauty should not come from outward adornment, such as elaborate hairstyles and the wearing of gold jewelry or fine clothes. Rather, it should be that of your inner self, the unfading beauty of a gentle and quiet spirit, which is of great worth in God's sight." 1 Peter 3:3-4

In Context

Wives, submit yourself to your husband that by witnessing your walk, your purity and reverence that if they do not believe they may be won into the faith. Your beauty should not come from outward adornment or elaborate makeovers but instead be a quiet inner confident beauty that reflects your heart which is highly valued in God's sight. This is the traditional way women who placed their hope in God have lived. They were submissive to their husbands like Sarah, who honored Abraham and esteemed him as her Lord. You are her daughters if you do what is right and do not give way to fear. Husbands, in the same way, be considerate to your wives as the weaker and as heirs in the beautiful gift of life, so that nothing will hinder your prayers. All of you, be like minded and loving, humble and gentle. Do not repay evil with evil or insult with insult. Instead repay evil with blessing, you were called to this that you may receive a blessing. In order to see a good life and enjoy good days, you must keep your tongue from evil and deceitful speech. You must seek peace and pursue it, God watches and listens to the righteous, but the face of the Lord is against those who do evil. Who is going to harm a do-gooder? But even if you are harmed, you will be blessed. Do not fear their threats and don't be frightened. But in your hearts, revere Christ as Lord. Always be ready to share why you follow Christ. But be gentle and soft in response that they may feel guilty when they slander you. It's better to suffer for doing good than evil. Jesus suffered too when he died to save us from an unrighteous life, he then rose from the dead to meet those that were dead in sin but saved through the flood waters of Noah, 8 in all. They were baptized in a way through the flood waters in which Noah and his people found grace. In the same way we are reconciled to God through baptismal, a pledge of alliance to God provided through the sacrifice of Jesus Christ to save us from sin.

Final Notes

Loving you is loving the Christ in you. Embracing that image instead of the one you think others want to see is always the way to go. God will bless you for being humble and trusting him to not only bless you but to fight for you as well. He has already died for us so we know there is no cost too large or heavy that he would not pay. Trust God to keep you in perfect peace as you prepare a way for his Spirit to travel.

Prayer

Lord Jesus, your beauty is beyond words. Your love is beyond comparison. Your ways are beyond understanding. Thank you. You are the rock on which we stand, the shadow under which we are comforted, the strong tower that protects us. Guide us, hold us, teach us to trust, obey, love and do as you desire us to do. Forgive us and help us to forgive others. We love you and thank you.
In Jesus Name. Amen.

My God is Able

"If it be so, our God whom we serve is able to deliver us from the burning fiery furnace, and he will deliver us out of thine hand, O king."
Daniel 3:17

In Context

King Nebuchadnezzar set up a high figure of himself and invited all of his top administration to the dedication. They all stood before it as they were instructed to bow before the image at every instance in which they heard a specific mix of musical instruments, it was a signal to worship the large idol image of Nebuchadnezzar. They were also told that if they did not fall down to worship, they would be thrown into a blazing furnace. Then some of the astrologers told the king that a couple of Jews in leadership would not bow to his idol or worship his gods. Angry and frustrated, he called the young leaders before him. "Is it true, Shadrach, Meshach and Abedneggo that you do not worship my gods or the image I have set up? Now when you hear the music, fall and worship and all will be well. But if you refuse, you will be thrown into a burning furnace and what God will be able to save you from my hand?" The young men told the king it wasn't necessary to defend themselves in the matter. In fact, they said, "If we are thrown into the blazing furnace, the God we serve is able to deliver us from it, and he will deliver us from Your Majesty's hand. But even if he does not, we want you to know, Your Majesty, that we will not serve your gods or worship the image of gold you have set up." This made Nebuchadnezzar so furious that he made the oven 7 times hotter and commanded some of his strongest soldiers to tie them up and throw them into the furnace. The fully clothed young men were bound and thrown into the furnace. Then the king leapt to his feet in astonishment. "Weren't there three men we threw into the furnace? Look! I see four men walking in the fire, unbound and unharmed. The fourth looks like the Son of God. Then King Nebuchadnezzar walked over to the mouth of the oven and called the young men that worshiped the "Most High God" out of the oven. So the young men came out and we're surrounded by the kings leadership (all that were ordered to worship his image). They saw that not one hair was singed, no scorch or smell of smoke and there was no harm to their bodies. "Praise be to the God of Shadrach, Meshach and Abedneggo. For he sent his angel to save them from the fiery furnace. They trusted him and were willing to give up their lives and refused to bow down and worship any other god besides their own God. Then the king made a decree that anyone of any language or nation who spoke negatively of their God be cut into pieces and their homes into piles of rubble because no other god can serve in this way." Then the king promoted the young men in the province of Babylon.

GOD IS ABLE

It was my Sabbath. As a new believer I was still transitioning from being an overt sinner to an overt believer and I was still using cocaine. I'd purchased a bag at lunch with a co-worker and we'd spent the afternoon high. I didn't do much of the bag though, just a little at lunch. I didn't want my friends to think I'd gotten too holy. As we got closer to 4:30 or 5:00, I couldn't wait do the rest of the bag. As soon as I got home, I went into my bedroom and began. Before you knew it, I'd done so much. I called my husband and asked him to get more before he got home at 5:30. He did and there we sat getting high. He didn't know I'd already done so much. Then it happened. I couldn't speak. My heart was racing. Tears first. Then snot. Then slobber. I looked at my husband in panic. I was beginning to overdose. I laid back on the bed and looked up. There was my Sunday School lesson. It said something about calling on his angels, but it moved me to begin praying. God please, I couldn't die like this. Not on a Sabbath, not with my kids in the next room. Please Lord, I prayed. Immediately, it felt like someone lifted a foot off of my chest. Air began to filter through and I was able to speak. I grabbed the bag of what was left and flushed it down the toilet. I thanked God for allowing me to live.

I didn't know if he would but I knew God was able to save me. I am so glad I trusted him in my own furnace, the hell I chose for myself. He was able to save me, just like those three Hebrew boys... just because I believed.

"Therefore I tell you, whatever you ask for in prayer, believe that you have received it, and it will be yours." Mark 11:24

In Context

Jesus sent two disciples ahead of him once they reached a certain city at the Mount of Olives. "Go into the city. You will find a colt that has never been ridden. Untie him and bring him here. If anyone asks why you do this, tell them the Lord has need of him," Jesus instructed. The disciples found the virgin colt in a place where two ways met (a crossroad) and loosed him. Someone nearby asked what they were doing and they responded as the Lord told them to. They brought the colt to Jesus and laid garments on him, then Jesus got on. They laid their garments and branches on the ground before him (making a straight way for the Lord to travel). All before and behind him cried aloud, "Hosanna, Blessed is he that comes in the name of the Lord. Blessed be the kingdom of our father, David that comes in the name of the Lord, Hosanna in the highest. And Jesus entered into Jerusalem, observing and then onto Bethany, where he became hungry. He was happy to spot a fig tree where he might eat. But he was disappointed to see the tree looked like it was bearing fruit but actually was not. He cursed the tree for pretending to be something it wasn't. "No man will eat fruit from this tree forever." His disciples heard it. Then Jesus went into the temple and turned over the money changers and sellers of items for false idol worship. He also would not allow any man to carry a vessel through the temple. Then he said, "Is it not taught that my house shall be called a house of prayer by all nations? You have made it a den of thieves." Then he began knocking over the tables. The chief scribes and priests heard it. They were astonished by him and began to plot his destruction. So Jesus left that evening and the next morning he and his disciples passed the fig tree without fruit. It was dead and leafless. Peter remarked, "Master the tree you cursed is dead and withered away." Jesus was certain, "Have faith in God. For verily I say unto you, That whosoever shall say unto this mountain, Be thou removed, and be thou cast into the sea; and shall not doubt in his heart, but shall believe that those things which he saith shall come to pass; he shall have whatsoever he saith. Therefore I say unto you, What things soever ye desire, when ye pray, believe that ye receive them, and ye shall have them. And when ye stand praying, forgive, if ye have ought against any: that your Father also which is in heaven may forgive you your trespasses. But if ye do not forgive, neither will your Father which is in heaven forgive your trespasses." When Jesus returned to the temple the chief scribes and priests approached him questioning his authority. Jesus responded, "I will also ask of you one question, and answer me, and I will tell you by what authority I do these things. The baptism of John, was it from heaven, or of men? answer me." But they were afraid to answer because their logic would be questioned and considered negative either way. Instead they responded, we cannot tell. Then Jesus replied, "Neither do I tell you by what authority I do these things."

Final Notes
God is capable of seeing you through any situation. Just trust and believe in him. Whether you are in a fiery furnace of your own design or put there by someone else, God has complete authority. He will move someone or something. He will command the commander. Don't worry about your situation, pray and believe.

Prayer

Lord Jesus, we thank you for every breath we take and every situation you have stepped in. Lord, help us to honor you with our hearts, believing you are not only able but that you will and that even if you don't, it is for the best. We desire to worship you in truth, not just with our mouths or for public affair, but truly worship you in our hearts dismissing all unbelief. We trust you. Help us to forgive that we may be forgiven. Help us to give to those that do not have. Help us to honor you in obedience. Grant us supernatural insight and strategies that will propel us to do more for the kingdom in powerful ways. Help us to experience supernatural growth and love. Help us to mature and become perfect conduits of your message, love and truth.
In Jesus Name, Amen.

DAY
31

The Everlasting Love of God

*"Look, I have inscribed you on the palms of My hands; your walls are
continually before Me."*
Isaiah 49:16

In Context

Those of you far away or on an island, listen and pay attention. The
Lord called me before I was born, named me inside the womb. He
made me sharp in word and action, a hidden weapon. He called me
his servant and proclaimed that he would be glorified in Israel. I
thought my actions were useless and just for show, but God justified
and blessed me. And now he that formed me in the womb asks me
to help reconcile his people back to him. I am honored in his sight
and he is my strength. Then the Lord told me that I wasn't enough
as his servant raising Jacob and protecting Israel. I will also make you
a light of nations, to be my salvation to the ends of the earth. This
is what the Lord, the Redeemer of Israel, his Holy One, says to one
who is despised, to one abhorred by people, to a servant of rulers:
"Kings will see and stand up, and princes will bow down, because
of the Lord, who is faithful, the Holy One of Israel — and He has
chosen you." This is what the Lord says: I will answer you in a time
of favor, and I will help you in the day of salvation. I will keep you,
and I will appoint you to be a covenant for the people, to restore
the land, to make them possess the desolate inheritances, saying to
the prisoners: Come out, and to those who are in darkness: Show
yourselves. They will feed along the pathways, and their pastures
will be on all the barren heights. They will not hunger or thirst, the
scorching heat or sun will not strike them; for their compassionate
One will guide them, and lead them to springs of water. I will make

all My mountains into a road, and My highways will be raised up. See, these will come from far away, from the north and from the west, and from the land of Sinim. Shout for joy, you heavens! Earth, rejoice! Mountains break into joyful shouts! For the Lord has comforted His people, and will have compassion on His afflicted ones." We think that God has forgotten or abandoned us, despite a mother who may overlook a child she nursed, it is not so with God. I have written you on the palms of my hands and your walls are ever before me. The people that build you up rush to do so while those that devastate you will soon be gone. Pay attention and look around, your children will surround you like jewelry and you will wear them as a new bride. Your waste land will be too small for the inhabitants and those who swallowed you up will be far away. Yet as you listen the children you weren't able to bear will say, make room this place is too small for me. In your heart you will ask how this was able to occur? I was left to defend myself without help... how could I birth? Thus says the Lord God, "Behold, I will lift up my hand to the nations and raise my signal to the peoples; and they shall bring your sons in their bosom and your daughter shall be carried on their shoulders. Kings shall be your foster fathers and their queens your nursing mothers. With their faces to the ground they shall bow down to you and lick the dust of your feet, then you will know that I am the Lord. Those who wait for me shall not be put to shame. Can someone take a lion's prey or snatch a captive from tyrant rule? Surely, this says the Lord," Even the captives of the mighty shall be taken and the prey of the tyrant be rescued, but I will contend with those who contend with you and I will save your children. I will make sure your oppressors eat their own flesh and they shall be drunk with their own blood as with wine. Then all flesh shall know that I am the Lord your Savior and your Redeemer, the mighty one of Jacob."

GOD IS FAITHFUL

Wow!!!! I am dancing up a storm because I promise you that if you are faithful over a few things God will elevate you.

I have been serving the community for years. I have also been working with clients that serve the community. In 2013, I heard God pushing me to take my business seriously. I owned Moore Marketing, but only served from a place of client need, not to sustain life. After

God's nudging, I developed processes and began to market myself. God seriously blessed me that year with outstanding client successes and I wanted to say "Thank You" with an amazing first fruit. I announced it on Thanksgiving Day. I started a program for women regarding self esteem. I strongly felt that this what God wanted me to do and I was obedient. That first year I was strongly encouraged by many of my national friends who vowed to contribute and help in any way. Gifts poured in from around the nation. Later in the year I felt God nudging me to start an etiquette class for my daughter and her friends. Then a boys leadership class. Then God pushed me to write a book. Then another book. Mind you, none of this was free and in between all of these projects, I got laid off from a television station as the matketing coordinator and God challenged me to go full-time in my business.

Every time he pushed me, he asked one question: Do you trust me? Of course I did. He'd saved my life more times than I could count when I didn't care about anyone but myself.

Now, when everything has changed and I was giving back in a dynamic way, I definitely trusted him. Most of the time I made my dreams come true on the whispers of prayer. No big financial backer came, no miracles... but God gave me outstanding clients. I became a campaign manager for a local candidate that won with 73 percent of the vote. One of my clients was featured on a national television show. Another client was a congressional advisor who'd overcome cancer twice. I have been blessed!

Nothing was easy though. I'd been betrayed by friends (one actually left me and all of my volunteers and two teens stranded in Atlanta), betrayed by clients, betrayed by myself (choosing purpose over bills and suffering without utilities), lost my car keys and totaled my car... but God was there through it all. I never became bitter but I did see anger, sadness and depression. In my wilderness, I continued to have faith. I continued to praise. I couldn't see my way through but I knew God was making a way.

By the end of this year, I will have authored 8 books, taken both of my teen leadership programs national (Dallas, Atlanta, Chicago,

LA) (She's a BOSSE is international) and developed a strong local and national brand for Moore Marketing and Communications. I am blessed. God is doing amazing things for me and I am grateful.

"One who is faithful in a very little is also faithful in much, and one who is dishonest in a very little is also dishonest in much."
Luke 16:10

In Context

Jesus told the story of a rich man with a manager accused of stealing. He approached the man and asked about the accusation and informed he would no longer be his manager. The man was in a conundrum because he lacked the skill set for other means of work. Instead, he called each of his masters creditors and asked them to share what they owed. He instructed each to take their invoice and write less on it. This made his master happy and he considered the stealing manager wise because he knew how to take care of himself. Street smart people are smarter than law abiding citizens in this regard. They are on constant alert, surviving by their wits. Then Jesus told them that he wanted them to be smart in this way as well, but for what is right and using adversity to spark creative survival. Concentrate your survival on the bare essentials, so you will live well. Jesus continues: "If you are honest in small things, you will be honest in big things. If you are dishonest in small things, you will be dishonest in large things. If you are dishonest in small jobs, who will put you in charge of the store? No worker can serve two bosses: he will serve the one and hate the other. You cannot serve God and money. When the Pharisees heard this they rolled their eyes and dismissed his words. "You are masters at making yourselves look good in front of others, but God knows what is behind the mask. What society calls monumental, God calls monstrous. God's law and prophets hit their peak in John, now it is all kingdom of God and spreading the gospel to all men and women. The sky will disintegrate and the earth dissolve before a single letter of God's law wears out. You cannot cover your lust under the law of marriage or divorce. There was once a rich man dressed well in expensive clothing. A poor man named Lazarus, covered with sores had been dumped on his doorstep. All he wanted was to get a meal of scraps from the rich man's table. His best friends were the dogs who came and licked his sores. The man died and went to heaven. He rested in the lap of Abraham. The rich man also died and was buried. While in hell the rich man looked up into heaven to see Lazarus in Abrahams lap. Then he called to Abraham and asked for mercy. He asked if Lazarus could bring him a sip of water. He claimed he was in agony. Abraham responded, "In your life you had good things but in his life he had bad things. It's not like that here, he's consoled and your tormented. Besides there's a big chasm between here and there and no one can cross from here to there from there to here. Well father, he responded, " Please send him to my five brothers so that they don't end up where I am." But Abraham responded, "They have Moses and the prophets to share the truth with them." The man said, "I know but they are not listening. If someone came back to them from the dead, they would change their ways." Abraham said, "If they aren't convinced by Moses and the prophets, they won't be convinced by someone who rises from the dead."

Final Notes

God has not forgotten us. He knows everything about us. He will not allow us to come to shame. Our job is to believe and trust him that everything will change. We are to creatively live and well in the face of adversity. We are to be faithful in a few things that we might be trusted with more. God is faithful and he will do as he has promised us he will.

Prayer

Dear Lord, as we embark on our final prayer we are reminded that we have not been betrayed by you. That your silence in our wilderness is just a test to see if we are ready to journey into our promised land. Thank you for clarifying that a man cannot serve money and you. That we must choose which is more important. We know that is you but if we ever waver in belief God please push us back along your path. Thank you for the blessings you are bestowing and arranging as we speak. Thank you the dangers blocked as we speak. Thank you for the angels encamped around us in protection. Thank you for faith to believe another day, another hour, another moment that you are real and died to save us. Thank you Lord your everlasting love.

In Jesus Name, Amen.

Into the Promised Land

"Hear, O Israel: Thou art to pass over Jordan this day, to go in to possess nations greater and mightier than thyself, cities great and fenced up to heaven."
Deuteronomy 9:1

In Context

Moses has just received the Ten Commandments and is coming down from the mountain. He responds... Today is the day you enter your promised land. This is a large land with fortified cities. I am going ahead of you to clear out the people, the strong people, that own it. I will do this quickly, just as I promised. Don't think this is because you are so good. You are stubborn and complained the entire time you were in the wilderness. You made God so angry, he wanted to destroy you. Kicked and screamed since the day I brought you out of slavery. When I was on the mountain 40 days and nights, I fasted from food and water. After God gave me the Ten Commandments, everything he spoke to you word for word at the mountain. When it was time for me to return, God instructed I do it quickly because you were already destroying and turning from everything he taught you. God wanted to destroy you and start over with a bigger and better nation. By this time the mountain was blazing with fire as I carried the Ten Commandments written by God's hand. Then I could see you! You'd already made an idol created by your own hand to worship instead of God. I threw down and broke the Commandments in your sight. Then I fasted another 40 days and nights for you. I prayed for God not to destroy you. He had a blazing anger with you and Aaron. He listened, to me

and Aaron! I prayed for Aaron too. I destroyed your idol, burned it
and threw the ashes into the stream. There were several additional
times you made God angry, time when you infuriated him. This last
time, God told you to go and possess the land but you were afraid.
Rather than trust him, you disobeyed him. You made him angry but
I prayed for you. I prayed, "My Master, GOD, don't destroy your
people, your inheritance whom, in your immense generosity, you
redeemed, using your enormous strength to get them out of Egypt.
Remember your servants Abraham, Isaac, and Jacob; don't make too
much of the stubbornness of this people, their evil and their sin, lest
the Egyptians from whom you rescued them say, ' GOD couldn't do
it; he got tired and wasn't able to take them to the land he promised
them. He ended up hating them and dumped them in the wilderness
to die.' They are your people still, your inheritance whom you
powerfully and sovereignly rescued."

Final Notes
Even though we chose not to trust God to bring us into our
promised land, disobeyed him, disrespected him with complaints
and distrusted him when he held our hands... we are blessed. God is
love and his mercy endures forever. His anger is but for a moment
but his favor is for a lifetime. Thank God for those interceding for
you, because their prayers have blessed you and thrust you into your
promised land - one you don't deserve but will undoubtedly possess.
Praise God! He is faithful.

Prayer
Most Gracious and Heavenly Father, thank you!
Thank you for loving us in spite of us. Thank you for your blessing
and faithfulness. Thank you for bringing us out of Egypt. Lord
before we possess anything, please forgive us and help us to forgive
those that have trespassed against us. Lord, help us to obey you
and trust you - doing all that you instruct us to do.
In Jesus Name, Amen.

About the Author

Stephanie D. Moore

Young Author with a Heart
Full of Passion

As a young lady Stephanie was molested by a friend of her family. In high school, she witnessed a friend die as she held his hand and prayed for God to spare his life. As an adult, Stephanie was a victim of a violent acquaintance rape. Subsequently, she struggled with personal demons. When she discovered the power of God and his word, her life was forever changed. I Give God ALL the Glory! He is and will always be the head of my life. He is my joy, my strength, my everything.

Stephanie D. Moore was born in Muskogee, Oklahoma. She graduated from Putnam City North High School in 1994. She was married in February of 1996. She is the mother of 3 beautiful daughters, Dallas, Brooklyn and Kaylia. She graduated with her Associates in Technology with an emphasis in Visual Communication. She holds several design and technology certifications and has won numerous awards in that area. Stephanie has worked in television, print and web media for more than 10 years.

stephanie d. moore

helping you
build your brand
with excellence

moore@stephaniedmoore.com
(405) 306-9833

Owner of Moore Marketing and Communications. Her company serves in the following areas: strategic marketing plans, public relations, writing, print and web design. She recently served as campaign manager for Oklahoma State Representative Jason Lowe, securing 73% of the vote in his district on November 8, 2016.

She's a

BOSSE

A Beautiful Oasis of Success, Style and Elegance

Since 2013, Stephanie has created and sponsored teen etiquette and leadership programs for young ladies and young men. The young ladies program is called, She's a BOSSE (A Beautiful Oasis of Success, Style and Elegance) and the young man's program is called, Grindaholix: Young Men on the Rise.

GRINDAHOLIX

151

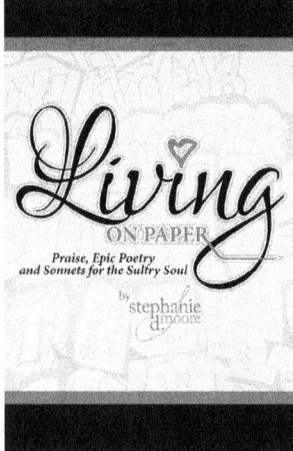

She's a
BOSSE

A Beautiful Oasis of Success, Style and Elegance

Leadership & Etiquette Clinique

For Young Ladies Ages 12 - 17

405 306 9833
ShesABosse.com
ShesABosse

LEADERSHIP & ETIQUETTE CLINIQUES
Oklahoma City, Dallas & Atlanta

Young Ladies will learn from Elite Leaders!
Grammar & Non-verbal Communication
Hygiene, Beauty, Fitness & Fashion
Professional Headshots (Digital)
Education, Entrepreneurship & Economics
Formal Dining Etiquette
$25 Gift Card will be given away Each Evening!
One Young Lady will Win a Laptop or Tablet!

Cost is $75 for all Four Classes!

LEADERSHIP & ETIQUETTE
FOR YOUNG MEN

GRINDAHOLIX

YOUNG MEN ON THE RISE

WHEN EVERY DECISION COUNTS
FOR YOUNG MEN AGES 12-17

GRINDAHOLIX: YOUNG MEN ON THE RISE

Who We Are:
Grindaholix was founded by Stephanie D. Moore of
Moore Marketing and Communications to benefit
African-American young men of single parents in low
income areas. The organization was founded in 2013.

Stephanie believes that a woman can't teach a young
man to become a man. For this reason, Stephanie
partnered with a close friend and psychologist that
specializes in treating young people from abusive
households to facilitate and guide the young men
through each leadership course.

What We Do:
Grindaholix partners with African American male business
owners, professionals and entertainers to impart wisdom
in a serious, yet relatable atmosphere designed to inspire,
motivate and encourage young men to become more.
We have a criteria for leadership and a foundation of
prayer and trust in God.

How It Works:
Classes are spread out over 4 Weeks or 4 Days,
depending on the market, in which various topics of
discussion are shared in the following order:

WEEK/Day 1 - Etched in Greatness: Foundation, Character & Choices
Trusting God and the Importance of Prayer
The Character of a Man
Tough Decisions - Grammar, Attitude, Actions, Intelligence & Perspective

WEEK/Day 2 - What You Can't Control: Race, History & Lineage
In the Absence of My Father or Mother
What You Must Know as a Black Man
Understanding You are Not Your Circumstance
Professional Head Shots with Photographer

WEEK/Day 3 - Mentally Fit: Economics, Education and Entrepreneurship
Get Your Money Right - Economics, Investments and Credit
Education 101: Are You Investing in Something You Can't Lose?
Entrepreneurship: Teen Entrepreneurs and Adult Business Men Share Critical Truths
Economic Board Game with Mark Johnson - What IS Money?

WEEK/Day 4 - Dinner with My Reflection
Formal Dining Etiquette and Dinner with Men Sitting Across from Each Young Man
Keynote Speaker: Chasing the Dream: Entertainer, Judge, Doctor or Respected Politician
or Successful B.O.
Essay Contest for Laptop & Professional Head Shot Reveal
Certificates of Completion

Every week, we give away a $25 Gift Card to Foot Locker to the young man nominated
for the Leadership Award by his peers. The Final Week we give away a laptop to the 1st
Place Essay Winner.

MARK JOHNSON
Financial Expert, Real Estate Investments,
Business Owner, Public Speaker & Mentor

THE CRITERIA OF A LEADER
I work hard.
I am disciplined.
I am honest.
I am a good friend.
I am a leader, not a follower.
I trust God.

www.ingramcontent.com/pod-product-compliance
Lightning Source LLC
Chambersburg PA
CBHW061727020426
42331CB00006B/1123